LOUISIANA NOTARY EXAM
SIDEPIECE TO THE 2020 STUDY GUIDE

Louisiana Notary Exam
Sidepiece to the 2020 Study Guide

Tips, Index, Forms —
Essentials Missing in the Official Book

Steven Alan Childress

QUID PRO BOOKS
New Orleans, Louisiana

Published in 2020 by Quid Pro Books.

ISBN 978-1-61027-405-0 (pbk.)
ISBN 978-1-61027-406-7 (ePUB)

QUID PRO BOOKS
5860 Citrus Blvd., Suite D
New Orleans, Louisiana 70123
www.quidprobooks.com

This information is provided to aid comprehension of notary practice and procedure, and of the Louisiana notary examination and its official study guide, and should not be construed as legal advice or the practice of law. Please consult an attorney for inquiries regarding legal matters. For information on how to contact the author about this guide, see the About the Author section at the end of the book.

Publisher's Cataloging-in-Publication

Childress, Steven Alan.

    Louisiana Notary Exam Sidepiece to the 2020 Study Guide: Tips, Index, Forms—Essentials Missing in the Official Book / Steven Alan Childress.

        p. cm.

    Includes annotations, forms, and index.

    Series: *Self-Study Sherpa Series*, #1

I. Notaries. 2. Notaries—United States. 3. Notaries—Louisiana. 4. Notaries—Louisiana—Handbooks, Manuals, etc. I. Title. II. Series.

KF8797 .C35 2020   2020818553

Second printing: March, 2020.

Contents

1

Introduction: "Where's the Index"?

The Louisiana notary examination is famously challenging. Still, everything you need to know to pass it is found somewhere in the state's official study guide.

Sort of. The content is all in there, true, but the organization and functionality of the guide—currently named *Fundamentals of Louisiana Notarial Law and Practice*—are notoriously nebulous. So the details are inside but hard to find, harder to learn than necessary, and missing some essential parts of any textbook—especially cross-references by page number and even a subject-matter index.

It's almost shocking that a book meant to be used in a time-pressured open-book exam omits the index. It's hard enough to learn the concepts and details without one, but especially difficult to find specifics during the exam itself. In a real sense the actual exam is a scavenger hunt for facts, some counterintuitive. Is the Louisiana civil code really the Napoleonic Code? (no) May a notary serve as executor of a will she wrote and notarized? (yes) May an absent heir appear through an agent's power of attorney to sign a small succession affidavit? (no) Can a bank be a corporation? (yes and no; see p. 93 below) Is a notary disqualified for a DUI arrest? (no) Try finding that trivia fast in a 650-page book with no index.

The exam's much more than a scavenger hunt, of course. But it's *at least* that. An index would help a lot, both to take the exam and before that to learn key concepts. It's especially surprising that the index goes missing in the one book you're allowed to crack open the day of a five-hour exam with a 20% pass rate.

Couple that glaring omission with the relative lack of forms that notaries actually use in practice—examples of authentic acts, affidavits, powers of attorney and the like—and you get the feeling that the examiners want you to construct *on the fly* the structure of a valid legal document. They don't, but they don't make it easy either.

I'm not really dissing the book. It's carefully written by leading authorities to be informationally complete, to be used fairly and uniformly the day of the exam, open-book. The content is impressive and interesting. The explanations are clear. It's such a profound resource that you'll find it on the shelves of every responsible law and notary practice, often in multiples years shown by a rainbow of covers (last year's was yellow; you need the bright *red* one). The answers to the 80-or-so questions you'll face on the exam are found in *Fundamentals*; the examiners don't make you, technically, depend on any outside resource. But the fact remains that almost all test-takers need help. The exam's just that hard.

Why did they leave out the index? A few years ago the book *had* one, if incomplete; but they've *removed* it! Even further back in time—when it was named the "Study Guide"—it was full of sample forms and acts, helping readers visualize the documents they were learning to draft. My guess is that the move toward an all-open-book test (initially it was closed-book, then one part was open, now yours is open fully) and an all-multiple-choice one (originally you'd write out acts and mortgages freehand) necessitated making the resource less useful the day of the exam. Or at least *perceived* to be one that could be taken just by going in with a book and its index (btw, a fullproof fail tactic). I think they believe the exam is fairer for all if the book doesn't give away too many answers by telling you where in the book to find the exact rule they're testing.

A more cynical answer is to observe that the default position for a notary in Louisiana is to be an attorney first—in fact in many civil law countries (and Puerto Rico), *only* lawyers may be notaries. Our state may be generous in creating nonlawyer-notaries and vesting them with many powers that in any other state would be the illegal practice of law, like drafting wills and donations. But in essence nonlawyer-notaries are treated as the exception, not the rule, so it feels as if the exam is hard so that notaries without law licenses remain a relative rarity in the profession.

That may be wise policy for all sorts of non-cynical reasons, but the result seems to be the consistent 15 to 21% pass rate (for most exams after 2011) even as the number of exams per year increased and the format became open-book with no written component. Be thankful it's not December 2010, when 14 of 602 takers statewide became notaries (2%, down from 5% that July; gulp). While practically all lawyers who wanted to become one did, for a small fee and an oath of office.

Anyway, the text now *feels* a little like what hardware designers call *crippleware*: a product like a computer chip or car that is kept sluggish by a simple switch, while the costlier souped-up model merely activates the switch. The red book's not, to be fair, "crippled" in its present form. But it's missing some relatively simple switches to make it much more functional.

There's no substitute for studying hard and reading the 2020 study guide closely enough that your mind becomes at least a general index. This book doesn't claim to be a shortcut to passing the exam. But the day of the exam will be less head-spinning, to say the least, with some key components like a detailed index added to the book. The process of annotating the book is educational in its own way. And the studying along the way will make more sense, and be more efficient, with help beyond the red book.

This book also doesn't really replace an organized course of study such as a private prep class or study group. It's not a workbook and outline (Fred Davis's are rightly famous and useful) or an interactive resource like others helpfully offer through classes or study materials. Some courses are online (Shane Milazzo offers a very good, engaging one), some are by written instruction and interaction, and some are classroom-driven: most of these are offered privately while a few are part of a college program.

Students learn best by more formal study, concepts explained orally, or intensive self-study in extra resources—better than reading one study guide on their own. Taking practice exams is very helpful, too, so classes or workbooks that offer those are good. This book is meant to be a companion to the study guide and, we hope, an additional reading to be assigned or recommended in those courses. That's why we made it affordable compared to them.

But a close review of the Secretary of State's database of private prep course reveals the scary news that, of the ones that even disclose their recent pass rates, most have success not far above the 20% state rate (but see some named above). This doesn't make them a waste at all—the same students without the instruction likely would fail at a higher rate—but it does caution that organized coursework is—I'm full circle here—no substitute for studying hard and reading the study guide more than once. Loyola's prep course website says it well: even for a 16-session course held February to June, "Please note that successful preparation for the exam will require extensive reading outside of the classroom."

One program is not enough. The official textbook is not enough. This guidebook isn't either ... but we hope it helps pull the other resources together and makes exam prep more sensible and organized. At the very least, the *one weird tip to a fatter wallet* shared at the end of ch. 4 about filing fees could save you over a hundred dollars, paying for this book and part of a prep course.

In addition to providing the essential missing material to be reviewed and inserted into the exam's open book, this companion guide also shares tips for prep and for exam-day, commonly tested subjects, typical mistakes, and conceptualizing the all-important authentic act and other forms—all keyed to the 2020 study guide. The much-tested notarial testament and community property are explained and illustrated. The goal is to make sense of an exam that, more and more, asks you to approach a question by finding an answer that touches on several different parts of the permitted book.

For what it's worth, I'm in a relatively distinctive position to comment on the process of becoming a Louisiana notary. I've taught law and Louisiana bar review for years, and studied the civil law notary for my course on comparative legal professions. I'm a lawyer who has practiced—but, like very many law profs in our state, hold my law license elsewhere. Yet I wanted to become a notary and offer such services in my university and outside. The Secretary of State doesn't care that I'm a California attorney (nor should he): courtesy appointments are for Louisiana lawyers. I'd have to take that daunting exam. I had a headstart in law, but I still needed to study that book carefully to get the notary details they test. I found it helped me a lot to create and use an index. I found it essential to write down acts and legal forms just right to be able to answer questions from the "scenarios" they examine. I took lots of practice exams.

It's admittedly odd for an attorney to prepare for and take this exam. Louisiana lawyers don't, so now I teach a continuing legal education unit to them that fills the gaps of how notary practice differs from law practice. As far as I know, all the teachers of notary exam prep are either Louisiana lawyers, so didn't take the exam, or nonlawyers who took it when the exam was in a very different format and the study guide was differently organized. I hope my sweating through the *actual* format and content that's tested nowadays, using the current form of the study guide, makes this a fresh and instructive sidepiece to other prep resources. You decide.

This book is also meant for new and existing notaries—including attorneys—who may find useful its practice advice (ch. 19) and "big picture" on the four notarial A's and the structure of wills (ch. 7-11), as well as visualizing the will's relation to community property (ch. 17). Most of all, many practicing notaries buy the new *Fundamentals* edition each year, and consult it for the many acts and areas of law that come before them. They may want an expanded list of acts required to be in authentic form (p. 54 below). They could use expanded cross-references. At the least they may appreciate having an index to the study guide, especially since the vital information on a topic is often found split across two or more parts of it.

2

Why Become a Notary Public?

To pass the exam, you have to be truly committed to the process. It helps to know in your core why you want to become a notary. The answer shouldn't just be that a boss suggested a raise if you get that commission, or a non-Louisiana company thinks being a notary is no big deal and is asking you to do it (a point suggested to me by a former Jeff Parish notary examiner, Karen Hallstrom). Or that it sounds like fun. I think it *is* fun, but that's not enough incentive to study extended hours beyond what is required in a prep course or seems normal for a professional exam.

But I did want to mention that there are many good reasons to become a notary, beyond the obvious job advancement or expanded responsibilities in an existing career. In career terms, another reason is public relations and client (or customer) development for yourself, apart from its positive impact on your specific job status. Having the seal draws people to you, at home or in the office. And those people perceive you, rightly, as a trusted professional for whom they can see future work in other spheres and give referrals to others. Most businesses kill for foot traffic; being known as a notary is a magnet for those feet.

There are also several new job openings and lateral moves available for those who are commissioned statewide as a notary, as you'll be. You can find work in real estate, law offices, government positions, automobile transfers and registration, and financial services that were not open to you before. One can strike out on one's own as a notary, not necessarily affiliated with for instance a real estate firm or a public agency, by opening a notary office yourself or by starting a mobile notary service. Especially coupled with other self-employment or services, as with a mailbox/shipping store or as a consultant to hospice care and assisted living places, this can be part of making an independent, professional living. (Luckily, it's also a way to earn fees without their being subject to self-employment tax, and isn't a "profession" in the sense of paying a license tax, see guide p. 44; yet there's no doubt that the work is "professional" in every important way.)

In my view, there's especially room for a mobile service that is effectively Uber-notary, at least in communities well serviced by ride-sharing or cabs. One complication for existing mobile services, as I perceive it, is that clients have a hard time wrapping their heads around the transportation add-on, which can be a (complicated) grid of locational areas or mileage from the place where the notary has their primary center (an office or home, for example). They don't want to pay the obvious transportation cost unless they know upfront what price range it's in, leading to complex websites that require potential clients to fill in web info such as location to get a quote. I'm guessing that's off-putting to some, or they fear gouging. But people instinctively "get" that transportation by ride-sharing is affordable and set by someone other than the notary. So the notary could make clear on the website what their rate for the specific service is (one signature? a bill of sale and transfer?), plus a charge that is some fair ratio (1.5 times?) of the actual Uber or Lyft charge incurred to the client, shown to the client from the phone, and doubled so as to pay for the return. They'd know that's the minimal transportation charge they'd pay, and it's fair. At the very least, even for a notary who likes to drive, there's room for rate-setting on the website stated in terms of typical ride-sharing costs. This is just another possible career aspect to becoming a notary.

More importantly, there are many non-career reasons to set this goal. Pride of accomplishment is real and valid, and a profession is understandably respected; it's not just a job. People have heard how tough the exam is (well, not friends from other states, where notaries are just functionaries). The work itself requires care, precision, and trust. Drafting testaments and powers of attorney for those who need them protects families and finances for many who might not have such an instrument just when they could use it most. You'll do a lot of good. And as with other professions, you can cause a lot of damage if you don't know what you're doing or you act unethically or unprofessionally. See the movie *Body Heat* for the harm one can cause by mis-drafting a will (and because it's a great film), in that case for violating a Florida rule similar to Louisiana's strict prohibition against (non-vulgar) substitutions in a testament.

Notaries in *common law* states (and common law countries like England) do require trust in one important way: that the person who's signing is properly identified. That function is performed by Louisiana civil law notaries, too, but they do so much more (see p. 53 in your study guide). The origin of the common law notary, beyond the church-witness function stated on p. 19, owes in part also to the need for the king to be sure the people who came before him were verified as who they claimed to be (say, not an assassin). It was a vital function, to be sure, but the identification-specialty this produced, quite unrelated to the practice of lawyers then, made the notary in effect the King's Bouncer.

You'll be more than that. The *civil law* notary grew out of a wider need in society for the verification, creation, and preservation of vital documents related to property ownership and transfers, family matters, and courtroom evidence (see ch. 1 and 3 in the guide). The civil law notary was always connected to law, legal documentation, and proof in ways that make the notary public historically linked to the profession of lawyer. We're not just ID-checkers (though much havoc results from skipping that step!). When you read the first seven chapters of the guide—about the history and functions of the civil law notary and of Louisiana's legal system—the main goal is to learn the terms, rules, and concepts for the exam. But read them with interest for what they say about the proud tradition you'll be joining and your vital place in the legal system.

Also, this is a position that you'll hold for life—all other states limit the term—at least if you report annually to the Secretary of State, stay registered to vote, and don't commit a felony. Plus it's one you can obtain later in life that will retain its value in your senior years. Most people don't go to med school or become CPAs at an age where it still makes sense to become a notary and the barriers to entry are more manageable. You won't need three years of law school or heavy student debt.

Finally, as challenging as the exam is, there's no real limit on how many times you can take it. You don't want it to be like the bar exam for *My Cousin Vinny* ("Nope, for me, six times was the charm."). But it *can* be. The point is that it's a hard enough exam that there's no shame in failing it, or retaking it. You can go into it with the mindset that the pressure, though real, is mainly internal and not life-altering if more than one time is a charm. No one should *plan* on taking it over—especially if such thoughts tempt you to "wing it" or not do your honest best. But you can certainly note parallels to the CPA process, by which all candidates know they must pass four separate exams. Even if the notary exam is the "same" exam instead of four separate parts, passing after three administrations is more efficient and doable than what the CPAs endure, if they even pass all four the first time.

Take some comfort in the fact that, as uphill as this exam feels, the effort is what *should* be expected of a "public officer" (p. 44) having such responsibilities and impact on people. Thinking "it's unfair this exam's so hard" only makes it harder to take it seriously enough to study each day, take extensive notes in your red book, take practice exams, use this companion guide to annotate your book in detail in preparation for the exam, and endure the five-hour exam itself.

At the end of it all, it'll be worth it.

3

Crucial, Inviolate Rules Using the Official Study Guide

The Secretary of State's website spells out the current rules for the day of the exam, including the prohibition on bringing food or drink into the test administration and the lack of a break in the five hours. (They do let you use the bathroom, which may have a water fountain, but trips don't extend your time.)

The website also lists the process to apply in advance for deviations from the fixed rules as accommodations under the Americans with Disabilities Act. Consider those rules well before going to the exam. They won't give exceptions on the fly. More on game-day issues later, in the next two chapters.

More immediately important to know way in advance are the rules that apply to the *Fundamentals* study guide itself, since that affects how you study and take notes for the exam.

Currently the exam is totally open book, in the sense that you can use the official study guide during the exam. But:

- It can only be the 2020 edition study guide for exams administered in 2020. You won't be able to talk the examiners at the door into letting you use an older book, for *any* reason. Everyone has the exact same *red* book on exam day.

- You can't insert pages or post-its, or otherwise supplement the book with loose sheets or attached material other than the original pages bound in the book. There's no pasting pages into the book, either. Proctors actually use the check-in process at each exam site to flip through each candidate's book and hold it by the spine to see if anything falls out. Even if the Secretary of State's office posts updates or errata to its website, presumably you should write them into the book rather than inserting a loose page.

- Tabs are allowed, but in a limited way spelled out on the Secretary of State's site. For example, the tabs must be the permanently-applied kind. Those are sometimes hard to find at office stores, which tout the repositional kind you can't use. They must be "clear" and a maximum of two inches. There can only be one tab on a page. While "clear" seems to include see-through but colored plastic tabs (as pictured in a link from the website), it's safer to use the uncolored kind on the off chance that the proctors at your site interpret "clear" in a strict way and ban your book (or at least make you remove the tabbing). Unless tabbing is important to your way of studying, there doesn't seem to be much advantage to it over the indexing and cross-referencing suggested in this guide.

- No electronic device or phone can be on (and if they suddenly buzz or sound, as in rebooting on their own, you get kicked out, no refund). So you best leave them in the car. No smart watch may be worn, whether on or off.

Still, that leaves a lot you *can* do with your study guide, to make it even more open a book:

- You can write in the book as much as you want to, in ink or pencil, in whatever colors you wish. The words and annotations so inserted are not limited to your own original thoughts.

- You can write on the blank inside-cover pages and other pages that have blank canvases, in whole or in part. The cover insides are especially good spots to add very important information that should be always handy, such as the skeleton of typical versions of authentic acts (see below at p. 48).

- You can use white-out over the print already in the book, to write over it and replace it with writing that's more important, organized, or usable to you the day of the test. To be safe, and not have trouble in the check-in process, I suggest that the painting-over process not be so thickly applied or used on so many pages that the physical appearance of the book from the side looks altered. Chapter 14 below has some specific suggestions on where to white-out, and what to replace it with.

- You can highlight or color-code at will, including using color markers along the edge to create a tabbing effect without physical plastic tabs.

In the process, you can turn the guide into what you want it to be, within the limits of these rules. It can become more functional than in its original form. Because of these rules, it makes little sense to take a lot of notes in a notebook or on a laptop, unless that's just a waypoint to adding the right ones, the best ones, somewhere into the book itself. You can't take the notebook in with you, or pages printed from your typed notes, so I don't recommend you waste much energy creating notes that can't be accessed—since you are perfectly permitted to take notes in the book itself up to its physical limits.

While making notes in the book, I suggest using a fine-point mechanical pencil with hard lead and a good eraser. You'll probably have some false starts and misprints along the way that are best changed easily. Even ink is all right, but be prepared to resort to white-out when you realize you have better points to make than the ones you started with. Such tips are detailed in ch. 5 below.

You could go overboard with the notion that the study guide is a canvas. But to some extent it really is that, and you can make it work for you.

4

Registering and Taking the Exam;
Important Exam Strategies

Registration and Pre-Assessment

The process of becoming a Louisiana civil law notary is spelled out for you on the SOS website, along with all the specific annotation rules for the study guide just discussed. The process picks up from the formal prerequisites of a notary found on pp. 61-62 of the red book, which must be learned not only to apply in the first place but also because they're testable requirements for all notaries. (See also the statutory appendix at pp. 591-92; you'll find details on all the requirements and regulations applicable to notaries, including the discipline process, in App. A.)

These qualifications include being 18-plus with a high school diploma or equivalent; in-state residence; registered to vote (for citizens); no felony record unless pardoned; and proficiency in English. Assuming you meet these minimums, which you verify in an account opened on the website (the "Application to Qualify"), you register and take the Notary Exam Pre-Assessment. That short reading comprehension exam has nothing to do with notaries or law. It's merely informational and advisory, but it's a good heads-up on reading weaknesses you may have that you realistically need to improve to pass the actual exam.

It takes about a week to get that feedback, then you can register for the exam itself (a month or more before its administration). In 2020, the exam will be given March 7, June 6, August 29, and December 5, a little earlier than last year. The March and August exams are given in Baton Rouge only, at LSU. These two are limited to the first 375 registrants—though they likely won't hit that ceiling immediately, and you can *see* the list of registrants on the SOS site, counting them to be sure it's not getting close to cut-off; beware, though, a surge of new registrants when test results are released from the previous administration, so best apply before then—a month after the last test date.

June 6 and December 5 have tests at LSU, too, and typically in Shreveport and Alexandria. New Orleans as yet offers no test site. The location is chosen for you by LSU's Center for Assessment and Evaluation (they say "where to report" like you've been drafted into the Army). And oddly you are informed of it by email not long before the test date, leaving you possibly unable to make plans for the trip until the last minute. Surprise! Oh, and several of these online steps cost you money, of course.

Exam Format and Test-taking Tips

The usual format is 75 to 80 questions, all multiple choice. Almost always, there are four options to choose from—not five, and not true-false as such. It is possible that some questions will be worded in terms of true-false options, but still leaving four choices for you to discern. For example, after a statement of facts or reference to a scenario or its library, the call of the question may be something like: "Which one of the following [four] statements is false?"

One format they've used makes choice D as "None of the above" or "All of the above." Yet the set-up to all questions (in bold face at the top of the exam) is to choose the "best answer." In exam-creation, it is not considered best practice to combine the general "best answer" instruction with a specific question that includes "None of the above," because there may be some reason that one of the other choices is not perfect but the others are very wrong—so, is "none" the best choice, or the imperfect but better option among the other two?

Or the general instruction confuses you with "D. All of the above," because you may believe that one of the options in A through C is clearly better than the other two. So the best answer might be, say, C. But none is actually wrong. Do you choose C as "best" or is "all" in fact best?

My best advice is that if the first three options are all wrong, even for some technical or picky reason, choose "D. None of the above," even though some are way more wrong than others. But if there's a fair case to be made that one answer is barely correct, if imperfectly stated, choose it rather than "none." And for "All of the above," use it even if one answer is not great. The good news is that they're likely to offer "all" in a situation where you can already tell that two of the options are correct. If you're right about that, it doesn't matter that you can think of a way to read the third choice as wrong; pick D.

Fortunately they don't use the "all" or "none" options too often in one administration. Hopefully if they do, it will be pretty clear what they want you to pick as the right answer, assuming you know the information tested or can find it in the study guide.

As suggested above, some questions are worded in a globally positive or negative way, such as: Which of the following statements is false? This format tests your ability to know (or find) choices from several places in the book, because the options don't have to be related in subject matter to each other. It may help to write "true" at the end of each option you think is true, reducing the options to the likely false one, because under test pressure it's easy to quickly mark the first statement that you're confident is correct—forgetting that you're supposed to pick the *false* one. I made that mistake on several practice exams until I made myself write "true" and "false" next to each option A through D, then went back to the call of the question above that to remind myself they're asking for the false one. And similarly where the call of the question is: Which of the following statements is true?

Even outside the true-false format with four options, many questions force you to use two or more different places in the book to answer the question as a whole. They can do this by breaking down the information *in the book* over two places; an example is the useful samples they give for appearances, inexplicably split between pp. 310-12 and 321-22 (see below at p. 41). Or the question itself makes you relate together two different rules to merge into one answer (say, the small succession is an affidavit; affidavits can't be done via power of attorney (p. 90 below); therefore, answer C is wrong because it's having an agent sign for one of the heirs on the succession form). Either way, study and mark up the book in such a way that you can quickly go to multiple pages, to read the right answer or to merge two ideas into one right answer.

The SOS site makes it sound like *all* the questions are based on "scenarios" (fact patterns of people doing things) which in turn rely on "libraries" of incomplete or incorrect forms. To be sure, they've moved in that direction more than in many years past. But the website's emphasis on this format obscures the fact that 15-20 of the questions are likely to be unconnected to any scenario or library of paperwork. They are straightforward questions about your knowledge of notary practice, Louisiana law in covered areas like property, court structure and jurisdiction, acts not supplied in a library, property descriptions, the civil law system, and even Louisiana history and geography related to the civil law.

These are standalone questions (rather than, elsewhere in the exam, a series of 10 to 15 based on one fact pattern). They are much like the legacy general-knowledge questions they used to test in a closed-book format. So you can't ignore the guide's introductory ch. 1-7 just because it'd be hard to test these subjects via a scenario. Be happy these are in reality low-hanging fruit if you can recall the right answer (e.g., that the signature is your "seal," p. 71) or, easier still, just know enough to locate and confirm the right answer that's virtually quoted for you in the guide. The exam would be harder if they meant it when they suggest every question derives from a complicated fact pattern.

Even when the questions *are* based on a scenario, and part of the group of 10 or so questions tested "under" that scenario, it's often the case that a particular question is only *loosely* based on the scenario—that the latter is just a jumping-off point to get you to define a term or apply a rule in a way that could've easily been asked without reference to the scenario. These feel like the scenario is more of an excuse to ask the question than a necessary part of it.

So it may be that, along with the low-hanging ones noted above, fully 15-20 of the actual questions (out of, say, 80) are pretty much standalone knowledge questions rather than analyze-the-scenario ones—despite the website's description. That doesn't mean they're easy questions, or all just trivia. But they can be approached in a straightforward way, especially using the indexing and referencing strategies shared further in this guide.

The scenario-based questions, too, make you use your ability to find relevant passages in the study guide and apply them to the inquiry at hand—here, in the form of a fact pattern or library of sample documents. *Recognizing* the issue raised by the fact pattern, and the type of form that is being referenced in the library, is a crucial skill. The answer ultimately will be found somewhere in the guide, but you won't know where to look, even after creating an index, if you don't "get" the question and identify the issue.

You have to see the big picture and understand concepts cold to be able to look in the right place—even to know what index term to look up. So this puts a premium on using the book and any prep course you take to *conceptualize* notary law and forms. For example, knowing what a personal servitude is, and that there are other types besides usufructs (though that's the main one tested), is more important than knowing their detailed differences, assuming you've listed differences in your guide and can locate the notes quickly despite test pressure. That changes the way you study for the test from how it used to be administered a few years ago.

When it was an exam of memorization, code-article identification, and form-writing, there were a lot of details to learn by heart. There's still a lot of that involved in the current administration. But you can study each page knowing that specific details they can test—for instance, that property records have to be filed in Orleans Parish within 48 hours, unlike the 15 days elsewhere (p. 57); or that there are only eight reasons you can disinherit a kid, pp. 445-46)—need only be learned enough to see there's an issue (if Orleans is mentioned in the question for recordation, that means something; if a reason is given for disinheriting a kid, you know it's got to be on the statutory list). Once you make an index to find the right spot, the tiny *detail* they're testing (say, this deed was filed too late for Orleans; daughter in the military hasn't talked to testator in years, but that doesn't let him cut her out of the will) can be found during the exam.

There's still a lot of memorization necessary, but it's about learning the frame-work and general terms well, which is simply a different approach from what worked in years past. Study time is better spent learning the forest and projected subjects they test—and turning the book into a ready reference—than in quizzing yourself on the eight reasons for disinherision, or the seven instruments that require a social security number. Turning the book into the reference resource is time-consuming, and this book offers no promise of less work, but the point is that the time marking up your book in an engaged way (more on that in ch. 12-13 below) is more productive than flashcards, memory drills, and note-taking out-side the confines of the study guide. Yes, it takes time to annotate the guide with a list of the seven social-security-number situations (p. 89 below); but you know if one comes up on the exam, and you've trained yourself to *recognize* the situation, you'll *find* their answer in a minute.

Our next chapter has more specifics on how the questions' format affects your study style and need to annotate the book. More exam-taking tips, especially about time-management, are also offered in the next chapter.

Exam-Day Process and Pitfalls

The day of the exam can be a grueling process, and not just because it's five hours long with no scheduled break. The test takes an hour or so to begin, because the check-in process for so many candidates is so long. (Even so, don't count on their letting you show up late just because the exam hasn't started.) Even the end of the exam takes a few formal steps that make you stick around when you'd rather be getting a drink.

Because no food or drinks are allowed during the exam, except if they provide a water fountain at any bathroom breaks you may take, you may have some difficulty taking medicines along the way. Be sure to disclose your need to do so to the proctors during sign-in, so it doesn't appear during the exam that you are eating and to be able to have access to water to take the medicine. If you need to be able to eat something during a five-hour stretch, for example because of glucose issues, be sure to apply well in advance for accommodations under the ADA. They won't allow it as a last-minute exception.

Also, because the actual administration of the exam, including sign-in, usually takes at least an hour more than the five hours of the exam itself, be prepared to go without food for at least six hours. Eat sufficiently, but not too much, before the exam—including possibly a protein bar or similar portable food just before the check-in period starts. At least at the LSU testing building, drink and snack machines are nearby during the fairly long wait before they organize the sign-in lines (divided by alphabet).

During the test, they enforce one important rule not given attention ahead of time: you're not permitted to write *in* the study guide. The exam booklet and scenario libraries provide plenty of scratch paper. They'll dismiss test-takers who write back into the official manual, believe it or not. It's likely their way to feel comfortable about reusing scenarios and questions without fear someone is spending the exam copying them for future students. In any event, you've spent months writing in it, so it could be old habit to jot a note as you take the test (for example, to remind yourself to come back to a place in the book). Make sure you do that only in the question booklet or other loose paper they give you.

As noted in chapter 3 above, they have strict rules on what objects you may bring into the testing room. Above all, don't have a device that could suddenly make a sound (even an *off* cellphone can decide to reboot and tell the world it's back on, or you may think it's off but it'll buzz in a way easily heard in the quiet of testing). They'll kick you out if you have an active device, even if you didn't mean to. Leave it in the car.

At the end of the exam, once time is called, stop writing immediately and sit in your seat until your packet of materials is checked and all loose papers are collected. Do not write anything, or fill in *any* pencil dots on the answer sheet, after time is called. It is lore that people have been excused from the exam and their answers not graded (after all that!) simply for filling in a few dots too late.

To avoid being at risk of such a tragedy, keep an eye on the time on the test center's clocks (not your own watch—leave that behind unless it cannot possibly sound). Devote the last five minutes to filling in one answer for every question asked. There's no penalty for a wrong answer, so there's absolutely no reason not to guess on the last few questions or even fill in dots without looking at the question if you have to, to make sure all questions get answered. You won't get counted off.

Passing Score

About a month later, or sometimes five weeks, LSU will send your result in a curt email. Officially the passing score is 75% of the questions they count (excluding some experimental or rejected questions they throw in, often to try out for future exams). But they reserve the right to adjust what passes after evaluation of all results and consideration of "post-test statistical analysis." This has meant in recent years that in fact a score of about 70% correct and above is passing. You can't know until you get your score, and they're only promising that 75% passes, but consistently they do wind up accepting many exams just below that score.

Receiving Your Commission and Saving on Fees

Once you pass, you are told the final formal steps you need to go through to be commissioned in your parish of residence. Once again the requirements, covered on study guide pp. 62-65, are not just steps to take but are statutory mandates to learn for the exam itself. Mainly you'll need to file with the Secretary of State an oath of office, proof of a bond or equivalent, and sample signature (your "seal"). Plus pay the SOS again, naturally. Congratulations!

The most typical "equivalent" of the surety bond is an Errors & Omissions policy ("E&O," to everyone). While the bond protects the Governor and is the minimum required, E&O goes further in insuring *the notary* against, well, errors and omissions you may make. It'd be worth the slight difference anyway (typically $8 more per year), but it actually pays for itself in a way not explained in the study guide or, as yet, by the SOS online....

Here's our "one weird tip" to save you $105 in filing fees during this process. In most parishes—all of them, as far as I could ascertain—the Clerk of Court charges that large fee to approve and file your proof of bond (which is a parish-wide documentation), in addition to filing your oath of office with the Clerk and all the registration and test fees you pay online to the Secretary of State. You then have to upload to the SOS site this proof you filed the surety bond in your parish, to get commissioned, along with another SOS filing fee. But the Secretary waives proof of bond filing if you instead upload the coverage/declarations page for an E&O policy from a reputable company (because E&O policies are issued state-wide). The E&O declaration must clearly show a five-year term of coverage, a set end-date, for it to avoid filing a bond with the parish.

So, since to the SOS, E&O coverage is "as good as" a bond (it's actually better)—and E&O is not filed in the parish, which must charge a large fee—the savings to a new notary is $105 less the $40-or-less higher cost of E&O. That pays for this book twice over. The savings continue every five years, too, because again you'll have to prove to the SOS you have some acceptable coverage. And the only acceptable way to prove that with a simple bond is by filing it, expensively, in the parish.

Either way, you still have to file with your parish a second copy of the oath of office—but that may not cost as much to file as a bond does. Here you can save a little by only paying a notary for one form, not two. You may think you need two originals (one for the SOS, and one for the parish), but you have *a month* to file the oath in the parish. Because the forms to receive a commission are best done by uploading to your SOS account, you retain the original to later file locally. Assuming you pay for the notary or other official to administer and verify the oath, this way you only have to do it once. More money saved. Plus your prep class teacher may offer to notarize your oath for free.

5

Study Strategies and More on Taking the Exam

Chapter 3 above set forth the examiners' rules about how you can alter the study guide and still use it the day of the exam. Because all notes you can use must be written into the book—and not put on loose paper or inserts—it makes sense that note-taking should be done as much as possible in the book itself. This won't work if you have too many notes, or ones that take too much space to explain. So there's a premium on *efficient* note-taking, reducing the key concepts and rules to bullet-points, sample forms, and visual guides like grids and flowcharts.

The examiners also allow you to highlight at will. But obviously a page full of highlights won't make any key concept stand out. You'll need to stay disciplined to keep from over-yellowing the page (or any color). Some marginal notes that actually explain something—such as the "AA" I next recommend adding to any discussion of a form or act that must be in authentic form—will be more useful the day of the exam than highlights.

Even more useful during the pressure of the exam will be cross-references and indexing that help you find the relevant point of the book (or a marginal note about it) that lets you answer the question. To that end, time spent marking up the book may help you less than committing to turning the glossary into a detailed index—as well as adding cross-references in the text itself where a form or context is discussed twice or more in the book, as often happens. It's my hunch that these multi-located rules are very testable for two competing but opposite reasons: (1) if they repeat it the same in the book, it's important, or (2) it's often true that the rule or key point is not repeated in two places, but rather only in one place is some *part* of it located and then the other place has *other* facets of the same subject. This means that you could find a place in the book during the exam where the subject is found, but only at the other spot(s) is the answer found to *this* question.

This examiners' trick requires that you extensively cross-reference the book and that your index be complete—not just have one reference to where the term or rule is "mainly" discussed. Further, the cross-references need to be by page number as much as possible, not just section numbers or headings. There won't be enough time during the exam to read through a whole section when you could've already identified the specific idea on a named page. My suggestions on expansive indexing and on cross-referencing are detailed in ch. 12 and 13.

In addition to notes in the book as it exists, and creating an index and other referencing, there's a golden opportunity (really, a white-out one) to create more room for forms and notes. Most prep courses and workbooks advise creating new real estate inside the study guide in convenient places. Too much of this will obscure the important parts of the book as it exists, or make certain pages so thick the proctors may think the book so substantially altered as to be disallowed. But they won't balk at your using white-out judiciously so as not to alter it in any observable way from the outside. They flip through it to determine whether you've inserted paper or attached notes, or used the types of tabs they forbid, as explained of their website. Mainly that's done by turning the book upside down, holding it at the spine.

So all you have to do is "paint" pages of the book just enough to write on: not too thick, yet not so thin that you can't read the words you write over the surface-text you've covered. The best way to do this is a few thin layers, with pausing and a little blowing perhaps, to allow drying between. Slathering won't work right.

It's become common advice in the prep world to paint your way to more room for notes and forms, so my main contribution is to suggest specific places in the current edition that are ideal candidates for covering. They're good for that because the material underneath is redundant or not particularly useful (such as copyright notice or title page), and sometimes because they are at a place in the book where they naturally belong. Other places are already blank canvases—such as the end of many chapters, or inside the covers—and can use some specific ideas for how they can be used. Some ideas for such locations are in our ch. 14.

Because the canvas is limited, it's best to write most notes throughout the book in pencil. That way you can erase notes you find you don't need and correct mistakes as you go. A fine-point mechanical pencil (0.5mm, or certainly no more than 0.7, such as those from BIC) works best. But for the new surfaces you've created with liquid paper, pencil works poorly, and you may want to use a fine-point ballpoint pen (0.7mm, such as Zebra or Pilot). Gel ink and other slick pens won't stick to this surface.

However you write it, the goal should be just enough information that you can *remember* broad concepts, organization, and key points from the notes, then *find* details and rules the day of the test as needed, as explained below. The student with the *most* notes won't necessarily be the winner. Even so, your judicious use of bullet-points and sample forms and acts requires more surface room than the book offers on its own, so the white-out tip makes sense.

Regardless of indexing and painting pages for more notes and forms, there's no substitute for reading all the chapters intently and repeatedly. Some more than others, as you can see from the "testable areas" discussed below (ch. 6). Some of the chapters seem to be in the book mostly to lay a foundation for other, more-relevant and testable, parts. For example, probably the main reason the study guide has such an extensive discussion of suretyships and bonds in ch. 16 is because they test your understanding of the requirement that *notaries* buy a surety bond (pp. 63-64 in ch. 7). And ch. 18 on mortgages is important to lay the foundation for its application to notary practice in ch. 21. Most of the actual questions are likely to be drawn from the part that most clearly relates to notary law. But it's still important to write cross-references to the more general discussion so that, on test day, you can easily find the related points made there if they do ask about them.

It may sound trite to say the best study tip is to study hard, but anyone who offers some magic solution otherwise isn't being honest with you. Fortunately, as the previous chapter introduced, studying hard is not about memorizing every rule or nuance—you're allowed to find those during the exam—but more about understanding the concepts, contexts, and organization of the study guide so cold that you know what you're looking for even if you don't have it committed to memory.

As an example, there's no need to know by heart all the instances in which Orleans Parish practice differs from the rest of the state. It's OK if you've conceptualized why that may be true, and made a handy list of relevant pages in your indexing under "Orleans." Answering any question that turns on the location is a matter of pinpointing it from the index. The same could be said for all the rules about when acts or forms need to be *recorded* in the clerk's office, not just signed at the notary's office. So the index added by our book lists multiple, detailed entries on "recordation." They tend to ask several questions, most likely three to five, that turn on recordation rules.

If anything, you may need to remind yourself during the test, rather than relying on memory, to search for a confirmation in the study guide of a rule you *think* you know. They can trick you by making the answer turn on some rule that actually has an exception, which you'd see if you just use your index to locate the relevant place. Or the actual rule is counterintuitive, the opposite of something you thought you've known all along, e.g., doesn't the Secretary of State appoint the notary? Is our civil code "Napoleonic"? (No and no.) At worst, a quick look confirms your memory was right and gives you confidence for the next question. You don't want to spend more than a couple minutes confirming the easier answers—save time for the rest of the exam—but having a thorough index handy lets you locate the low-hanging fruit fast.

You should similarly go into the exam with a plan for how long you spend on any one question. Commit to spending no more than three or four minutes even on the hardest question, mark your best guess, move on, and come back to that one if you have time. 300 minutes divided by 80 questions is 3.75. Some easier questions (that "heir" is used for an "intestate" testament) take far less and buy time, but you also may need time for a bathroom break or two and a water-fountain sortie.

Of course you won't waste focus actually timing each question, but you certainly can get a feeling that you're lingering on a hard one. It's better to return to it later than not to finish the exam, missing the chance at several closing questions. Meanwhile, though, fill in the dot of your best effort for those four minutes (you probably did at least eliminate some answers and so increased your odds), even if you think you'll come back to that one later. Don't make a habit of leaving blank circles along the way. You can change the answer if you're sure you did it wrong the first time around—basically, only if you see the correct answer in the book itself or you realize a clear reason your guess was wrong. Otherwise, leave your four-minute answer alone.

In addition to the standard tip not to linger too long on a hard question, ULL's Fred Davis has made the larger point that you don't want to fixate on a whole section at the start of the exam if it's bogging you down or freaking you out. Maybe the first 15 are a difficult subject-group for you (e.g., it's on sales and mortgages, which baffles you). So, simply start at Question 16, at a section (say, notary practice) that creates momentum. Everyone gets the same questions, but there are two versions of the test used in the exam room—called A and B, to prevent copying—with the questions in different orders. I'd add you probably should not skip too many individual questions as you go, but skipping a whole section of 15, to return with some wind at your back, makes sense.

On any one question, be sure to read all the answer choices and not fixate on the first one that looks right. More and more, the examiners emphasize that it's a search for the "best" answer, not one that is right in some technical or limited way. They consciously include a "distractor" that is OK as far as it goes, or partly right, but doesn't fully resolve the essential issue in the question—and doesn't count. It may be right for a narrow reason when the larger concern you can see they are trying to test by the question as a whole is not met.

To be sure, there are plenty of questions with only one right answer, and this dilemma of the tempting distractor at worst narrows you down to two decent options. So it shouldn't intimidate you too much. Just be aware of how they do that at times and the need to read all choices. This feeds back to my suggestion, above at p. 12, of noting true or false next to statements in A through D, to keep it all straight as you go.

As challenging as one section of the exam may seem, or the exam as a whole even, keep in mind that there's a decent margin of error to earn a passing score. Since 70% usually passes, and they'll have as many as 80 questions, you can miss around 24 questions and still pass. Knowing this should ease the pressure some, especially for any one question that risks bogging you down (say, a tough property description one). I recognize that not all of the 80 questions are scored, as some are experimental, but the logic of this *ratio* still applies: if all 80 counted, you'd need to get 56 right, and so on for smaller numbers.

This also means that in a section of 15 questions, and assuming five such groups (a total of 75 questions), you can miss *four* questions in each group and still leave room to miss a couple more here or there, and pass. You can set a realistic goal for any one question, or any one section, and not be overly intimidated.

6

Commonly Tested Concepts and Mistakes

Terminology and Definitions

Terminology is often tested, but usually not through such a straightforward way as repeating a definition from the glossary. It's useful to re-read the glossary and learn the definitions of legal phrases and other terms of art (and possibly use the short, handy, and affordable book *Louisiana Civil Law Dictionary* to nail them down). But mainly legal terms come up in an indirect way—by their application in a scenario that won't make sense if you don't know the glossary well. The examiners especially like to use words in the midst of a scenario that are hard to keep straight if you haven't studied hard those terms that differentiate the parties to a transaction, terms that aren't necessarily intuitive.

The most obvious set of legal terms that are mutually confusing and involve people involved in legal matters are: actors' roles ending in *-or* versus *-ee*. It is crucial to know, for instance, what a scenario means by mortgag*or* versus mortgag*ee*. Offhand you may think that the one who provides a loan to someone buying the house is the mortgagor; after all, they're the one making the loan that is the underlying goal of the mortgage. But in fact the mortgagor is the one making the mortgage, so that's the borrower and buyer in our example. Another confusing set is less*or* versus less*ee*. Which one's the landlord?

Really, though, the terms make sense if you can remember this one rule of thumb taught in law schools over the years: *-or* and *–er* mean the one who is *giving* the interest, property, or legal device. While *-ee* designates the one who *receives* it. You already know this hint when you use it in more common contexts you've used all your life. You already know employer and employee. Even if both benefit and both give something to the transaction, the one who gives employ-ment is the employer; the one who receives employment is the employee. Know-ing the easy terms, you can analogize to less-known pairs like lessor-lessee. The one who gives the lease is the landlord, called the lessor; the one who receives it is the lessee. Don't think for a minute that a tenant/lessee can dictate the lease to the landlord.

Another pair that's easy to see is grantor versus grantee. A grantor gives (grants, for example, an easement), while a grantee receives the grant. It's the same with payor-payee: the payee receives the money. Now just play the same trick on other paired terms that you don't already know or can't as easily figure out. So:

- Mortgagor gives a mortgage (and often is the only one who has to sign), while mortgagee takes it and is thus the lender. In the typical transaction, the mortgagor is the home-buyer. This pair is the hardest but most tested.

- Obligor gives an obligation (like owing child support) to an obligee (receiving payment)

- More examples are stated in abbreviated form below.

Also, you can remember the difference by noting that the giv*er* ends in the *−er* form (same as *−or*; ends in *r* like giv*er* does). While the word *receives* has two "long e" sounds in it, just like *−ee* (so, *receives* rhymes twice with *−ee*).

I hope this concept makes it easier to differentiate confusing pairs on the fly during the exam. But just in case, you could write, near the first glossary page, or anywhere easily found on test day, several of these:

> grantor=one who gives / grantee=receives the grant
> donor=one who donates / donee = receives donation
> m'or =borrower=home-buyer / m'ee=lender=bank
> lessor=landlord / lessee=renter
> vendor=seller / vendee=buyer
> creditor=gives credit to a debtor
> assigner=one who assigns / assignee=gets the transfer
> drawer=one who gives check / drawee=receives it=bank→then pays to payee

In addition to confusing pairs, there are other definitions that seem to be most testable, many listed below. If they're not in the glossary already, they should be inserted as part of your expanded index, as detailed below (ch. 12), adding cross-references in the book to where they are defined or applied (ch. 13). Such core terminologies include:

- Donation *inter vivos* vs. donation *mortis causa* (a testament or will)

- Donations that require authentic act vs. onerous donation vs. remunerative donation vs. "giving in payment" (*dation en paiement*)

- Cash sale vs. credit sale (act of sale with vendor's lien) vs. sale with mortgage

- Conventional mortgage vs. collateral mortgage

- Predial servitude vs. personal servitude

- Dominant estate vs. servient estate

- Usufruct vs. naked ownership

- Mandate vs. procuration

- Movables vs. immovables

- Authentic act vs. authenticated (acknowledged) act (ch. 11, below)

- Intestate vs. testate succession (ch. 10 and 17, below).

- Inheritance vs. legacy; heir vs. legatee

- Succession by affidavit vs. judicial succession (the one they stress notaries may not do)

- Community property vs. separate property

- Provisional custody by mandate vs. non-legal custodian's affidavit vs. designation of tutorship

- Corporation vs. LLC vs. partnership

- Act of correction by parties vs. act of correction by notary

- Point of beginning vs. commencing point (for property descriptions)

The most common of these ought to be learned cold, with no need to find a definition in the book. Searching the guide would instead be for finding detailed rules about it or applications of it.

Testing Recent Changes in Notary Law

Notary prep courses emphasize that topics that are very testable have had a change in the law the last few years. More precisely, these teachers say that they are subjects and rules that have had a change in the *study guide* in the last few years. Where the new edition deviates from recent ones, look to get tested.

This makes sense. If it's an area of change and upheaval, your antennae should be going off. I'll add my own conjecture that the most likely source of such test questions—if you are taking an exam early in the year—is not a very new rule changed in the newest study guide (the one you must use), but rather in the couple of years before that. I say this because LSU's office of testing works with notary test administrators to come up with fair tests, which would seem to require some vetting of and communication on individual questions before they are officially used on the exam. I doubt they have time to use this rigorous procedure for sudden changes reflected in the latest edition of the book, at least in the early administrations. It may be that changes that occurred an edition or two before would be ripe for use. If you do see a question on the exam that turns on some very recent change in the law, it stands to reason that question is experimental and won't count toward your score. If it's proven to be valid, it will become an official question later. But then it would seem likely that in administrations occurring later in the year, very new changes *would* be ripe for testing.

Even so, below are areas of law or the study guide that have changed in the 2020 red book. A fair list of the most testable developments from other years' guides (not necessarily the year the law changed) follows. You can anticipate that three to five questions will turn on one of these changes, which should be readily answered if you have indexed the topics well to find the passage that applies. You may also want to go to the text and highlight all new areas of law in a different color from other highlights, or write "NEW" in the margin. That could be a few points that act as low-hanging fruit for you.

The following doesn't list the entire page-range for the topic—just the first page.

New in the 2020 Study Guide

- 62: new emphasis that resident aliens can hold a commission even though they cannot register to vote; similar to the previous emphasis, p. 409, that non-citizens may inherit as an heir.

- 129: donations null by operation of law. The previous edition listed all the grounds, but now it explains each prohibition, not just substitutions and donating all property. Add to the list: reserving a usufruct? (p. 124)

- 175: four legal impediments to marriage; plus the new emphasis in 2019 that couples who move to Louisiana have a year to opt out of the legal regime just as pre-married couples do, p. 185.

- 189: parents, tutors, etc. may dispose of minor's property, or lease or encumber it, only with court approval

- 263: movable property is not susceptible to mortgage (instead, it's a UCC9 security interest), replacing earlier guides' statement that movables can be burdened by a mortgage. They've left it a little ambiguous whether a mortgage can finance personal property ("chattel," at common law) or movables, since they still mention chattel mortgages at p. 278, and imply on p. 283 that a mortgage may involve movables; still, the "right" exam answer must be that you can't mortgage movables (iPhone, car, stocks, CD, etc.).

- 295: to the list of acts needing authentic form, they added revocation of entire testament by testator, p. 441, though it would seem that it could be done via a new, olographic will that is, of course, not authentic. This is because art. 1608 requires that it just be "in one of the forms prescribed for testaments," pp. 440, 458, which of course includes the handwritten kind. It seems the answer they want, though, is that the whole testament is revoked by authentic act—or else they wouldn't have put it on p. 295.

- 395: the Act of Donation section is much expanded in 2020, consistent with p. 141, emphasizing that an authentic act may be required by OMV.

- 406: the explanation of *seizin* is added, though it was in glossary before.

- 433: adds limits on the notary's capacity to be a legatee (the will is still valid, but the notary takes nothing), consistent with p. 316, repeated on p. 434, and tested in 2019.

- 508: repeats that partnership contract need not be in writing, then notes situation to avoid collation where authentic act is required. Also adds this organizing contract *can* be in foreign language unlike for LLCs and corps.

- 511: section on "Purpose" is clearer than previous years (which left a sentence fragment to make it *really* unclear), but remains somewhat ambiguous, as discussed in our ch. 16 below.

- 532: expanded introduction on Building Contract Liens, and almost all of the next page, on notice to owner being required, is newly added. Then, most of pp. 534-35 is new, especially the clarification that it need not be a notarial act, the last two bullet-points for the statement's contents, and the filing requirement (it seems particularly testable *where* it's filed, and the requirement of more specific property description than street address).

- 556: the book is missing three pages at this point of material formerly in the book (and still in the table of contents), especially subordination of mortgages and verification of pleadings. This "change" may be fixed by the SOS website in an errata link, and is discussed below at ch. 7, re Affidavits.

- 591: section 191(A)(1)(d) clarifies "high school equivalency" to approved tests that are not just the GED. And p. 596 now omits several pages of the statute that allowed for provisional appointments of notaries and some terms applicable because of Katrina.

- 615: DeSoto Parish now has up to two ex-officio notaries, effective Aug. '19.

New in the 2018 or 2019 Study Guide

- 126: expanded discussion of onerous and remunerative donations, and addition to comparison of dation en paiement, p. 128.

- 164: new emphasis on 3-party acknowledgment of paternity, also at p. 526.

- 166: explanation of parental authority; and see p. 310 on appearance clause.

- 168: four ways to create a tutorship, including tutorship by nature.

- 229: power of attorney authorizing agent to buy or sell immovable must be express and in writing; earlier editions stressed the next sentence: the power to donate must be express.

- 271: partial release of mortgage by financial institution.

- 288: drafting pleadings, rules, etc. is off-limits to the non-attorney notary.

- 307: the discussion of *Dale* is important, because it cautions that disclaimers may invalidate the authentic act, undoing its formalities. Also p. 578.

- 314: the section on electronic signatures was recently expanded, but the last paragraph reminds us that most notarial acts are humanly passed before the notary.

- 319: costs of recording a sale of an immovable are borne (not born) by the buyer, unless the parties provide otherwise.

- 346: a *dation* may be a donation in disguise (requiring authentic act and donative intent) if the value of the thing donated exceeds the amount of the debt it extinguishes by over two-thirds (an issue tested July 2019).

- 362: the long section on Consumer Privacy is relatively new.

- 387: subsections (3) and (4)(a) are two new ways of "endorsement," and these two don't necessarily require a notary (the bank one needs at least an authorized officer, however, which may include a notary).

- 397: the documents listed as 7-10 are a relatively new addition. On p. 402, item 10 is new (OMV treats estates, living trusts, and DBAs as businesses). And p. 403 on sales and use tax is expanded, as is p. 405 on canceled sales.

- 414: escheat to the state is expanded; the section on Accretion is new, p. 415.

- 424: the 2017 case, *Toney*, cautions the literal use of the code-stated attestation clause. The "Formalities for Notarial Testaments" part is new, and spells out the code on deaf and blind testators, etc. (tested in 2019). The "What is a Legacy?" section starting p. 429 is expanded, and p. 431 has more on accretion (see p. 415), which seems testable. *Toney* is cited again on p. 454, requiring the testator to sign "his name" on each page—not just initials; and the surrounding matter on signatures is updated, too.

- 441: new case, *Harlan*, suggesting an invalid will doesn't revoke a prior will. And p. 446 has a new paragraph on electronic communications having an effect on disinheriting an uncommunicative forced heir by subsection (8); p. 449 emphasizes that testator may limit partition while heirs are minors.

- 468: the explanation of "pour over trust" is new, and was tested in 2019. The Class Trusts section on p. 481 was rewritten.

- 495: the small-succession ceiling was recently raised to $125,000.

- 504: partnership contract need not be in writing, but really, ought to be.

- 518: new mention of a "low-profit LLC"

Testable Issues by Subject Matter

Some larger issues are notable for how frequently they are tested, or otherwise are good candidates for coming up on a new test. One can predict, roughly, certain subject areas that deserve more study and cannot be known just vaguely before the exam. This estimate is based on several factors outlined in the next section (where I break down test-worthy issues by chapter, instead of topic), but primarily on what is generally known about recent administrations.

It's very predictable, for example, that testaments and successions will be tested, as it almost always is. It should be the subject you would study repeatedly, and again the day before the exam. In addition to points of emphasis already noted above in this chapter, here's what I observe to be the *top-10 subjects* ripe for extra study and detailed indexing or cross-referencing:

1. *Wills and successions, including small successions.* Ch. 24 and 27.

All four of the 2019 administrations, and plenty of prior ones, had an entire section of at least 15 questions on testaments, including a library of will-related documents. Not all 15 questions necessarily drew on the library document or actually tested a rule about wills—examiners can use the will to jump off to a related question such as property ownership or trusts. But still a dedicated group in the exam was about wills or successions. And questions in other sections of the exam could turn on wills without being labeled as such (such as the heir/legatee difference tested in a section called "succession by affidavit"). That makes for about 20-25% of the entire exam, some of the harder questions, related to testaments. It's almost as if a notary prep course should spend a quarter of the semester on the subject. They don't, because there's so much else to cover, but self-study should certainly aim for understanding it very well.

Specific subtopics are discussed in depth in our ch. 10 and 17. Suffice it to say that, beyond the mechanics and definitions of intestate and testate successions, and the formal authentic requirements of a valid will, the examiners may use a library document to force the candidate to show an understanding of how property is divided up among legatees. And how the normal process can be changed by a testator (as by disinheriting, or setting up a trust).

The testator may also control the disposition of their remains (through a notarial will, not an olographic one), p. 450. This subject was tested in both July and December, 2019, including a follow-up question on one exam about who gets to make the decision in the event the testator did not specify.

As for small successions, often called "succession by affidavit" because it is now possible to use the procedure for even a large estate if it's old enough, they can readily test the simple math of what's in an estate (in turn making you know what's separate property (our ch. 17), and that the 125k cap is for gross estate value, before debt). They may also test the normal requirement that the testator not have a valid will (if in-state), as well as the heirs that have to sign, or be notified of, the affidavit (or someone with knowledge if only one heir exists and no surviving spouse, p. 497). Don't forget that, since it's an affidavit, it can't be done by agents under a mandate. That's not intuitive, since absent heirs *are* part of the process—but their interest is satisfied by notice, not a power of attorney.

2. *Donations.* Ch. 10.

Acts of donations *inter vivos*, especially for immovables or related interests in land, make a good library document and scenario to analyze notarial law, practice, and statutory directives for an authentic act. Information is scattered through the book (not just ch. 10), making it important to index; it's tested enough that you'll also want to review it as a unit, bouncing around in the book.

Topics include: forms of donation (gratuitous, onerous, etc.); form *for* donation (proper construction of the authentic act, if required—and is it?); who may do-nate, and what; formality and timing of acceptance (in writing, but no longer needing authentic act, and that's *when* donation is effective, p. 137); recordation (p. 141); "magic words" of donative intent (e.g., "give," not just "convey" or "transfer," pp. 140, 455); different rules for donations of cars (pp. 135, 141 and 395); and ways in which donation *inter vivos* differs from a testament—such as that donations while living can be made via power of attorney (pp. 229-30), but testaments can't be (p. 421).

Proper construction and content of the act of donation is very important, but it's found at pp. 347-50, not ch. 10—so, index that subtopic, and cross-reference to it from ch. 10 in a few places. And no example form is given. The subject is tested enough that's worth the effort to write a sample act somewhere in the book and index to that completed form. At least review a completed donation, such as the one, below, in our ch. 18.

Recent additions to the study guide (in scattered parts of in ch. 10 and elsewhere) emphasize the different forms of donation and which ones must be authentic. They may test it as a bare question about definitions, or may offer a scenario (or a what-if change to a previous scenario), asking what kind of donation this is: onerous? remunerative? or instead a *dation*? In the process they may test your understanding of the manual gift (p. 135), and the definitional differences between movable and immovable (e.g., car vs. land, see pp. 82-84), and then corporeal vs. incorporeal movables (e.g., car vs. stock shares, pp. 83, 135). Even within incorporeal movables, rules differ if it's evidenced by a certificate or instrument.

All four exams in 2019 had extensive questions or a whole library on donation *inter vivos*, and two of these had a fairly extensive *dation* element in it.

3. *Other transfers and ownership of property, especially immovables, and related instruments such as mortgages and usufruct.* Ch. 9, 18, 21 and 23.

Beyond donations, transfers of immovables are done through sale or exchange. Forms of transfer include: cash sale, credit sale, bond-for-deed, exchange, sale with right of redemption, *dation*, and timber sales. They seem to test, repeatedly, an ability to identify which version it is from seeing a library example or from "magic words" in the scenario (e.g., a credit sale often has language of "vendor's privilege," "vendor's lien," or "owner-financed," p. 334). All of these forms have specific content and terms in their acts, detailed in the study guide, and may have "additional provisions for conveyances" (so, cross-reference a lot to p. 350).

And beyond transfers of interests in land, there's what kind of property interest it may be. A recurring area to test—with at least two 2019 exams having libraries and the others having several questions—is the very-civil-law concept of usufruct and naked ownership (ch. 9, but it also arises in aspects of several other chapters, such as the usufruct of a surviving spouse in ch. 24 (see below, ch. 17)).

Related to transfers of immovables are instruments secondary to the sale or conveyance, especially mortgages including collateral mortgages, and accompanying documents such as the promissory note. They used to test collateral mortgages a lot, but I get the impression it's not as heavily tested recently. Yet it's still important to learn all such documents that accompany a sale of an immovable and their differences in terms of who must sign; whether it's record-ed, and where; whether it's a negotiable instrument (and their relation to UCC9 security agreements); and whether it requires a paraph by the notary. It's crucial to keep straight all the parties to such a transaction, because now there's a lender who is also a "mortgagee."

A related testable area: which situations require, in the appearance, part of a social security number? It's important to write out such a list somewhere in the book and then index to it (gathered from the guide's scattered examples). See below, at ch. 15, for a complete list and suggested place to annotate your book.

Transfers of interests in movables may also be tested, such as questions based on ch. 23 about titled vehicles. They don't have the extensive notarial forms, and detailed content, that acts for immovables do. But OMV has its own quirky rules about the certificate of title, donations, and even what a name is (no apostro-phes, no Sr., no spaces, p. 402—just remember St. Andalone is STANDALONE).

4. *Trusts*. Ch. 25.

Although it often comes up not in a complete section but in the context of a different grouping (usually testaments or donations), it's easy to embed some trust questions into another section. A library document can include a will that creates a trust, or tries to. A property section can have a question of two on what-if-it's-a-trust. Recent topics have included: pet trusts (p. 479); who can serve as trustee (p. 465, including juridical persons); whether a trust is a juridical person (*no*, p. 463); the settlor as beneficiary (p. 471); and who owns the property under a trust (the trustee, unlike in common law states, p. 463).

5. *Appointment and regulation of notaries*. Ch. 7 and Appendix A.

This kind of background information (even "trivia") was a major part of the exam when part of it was closed book and tested "general knowledge." You'd get the idea from reading the SOS website that this section is abandoned, as if all questions now draw on a library or involve a scenario. Not so. The closed-book aspect is gone, but most exams seem to have about 15 questions that may be called a "legacy" of the old format, often in its own section though it could be fewer such questions spread among other parts. One can guess they would split the 15 or so between "notarial practice" and, less so, our #7 below on the civil law system. Know who appoints a notary (the Governor); eligibility for appointment (e.g., valid voter, no felons unless pardoned); their duties; who disciplines them; and for what. Notary practice includes the fact that a commission is parish-based (vs. statewide *jurisdiction*); the "de facto doctrine" (p. 67); duties of recordation (ch. 6, 7); and statutory directives in acts (pp.59-60). But the "practice of law" is forbidden (pp. 74-76, 288, 499). It's tempting to gloss over the early chapters as mere set-up to the heart of the study guide, when in reality several questions may test the backstories in our items #5 and #7.

6. *Recordation of documents.* Various chapters, as specified in our Index below.

The exam may be peppered with isolated questions (or parts of the A-D choices) that turn on requirements for recording a specific act—who does it, when, and where. These details would be hard to memorize but fortunately can be indexed well (see our ch. 12 under "R") and answered the day of the exam. If a question turns on whether and where a specific instrument is filed for registry, as for example the adult adoption tested December 2019 (it must be, but any parish's clerk of court will do, pp. 164-66 or p. 529), you should be able to find the recording rules somewhere where it's discussed (in this instance, both places, but often it's in only one of the two or three guide sections on a topic).

Even though there's unlikely to be an entire section on recording or filing of instruments (it's hard to make a library or scenario focus on *that*), many other topics raise additional recording issues, and the examiners seem to come back to that aspect again and again.

The examiners tend to test the notary's different time period to record acts involving immovables depending on whether the property is located in Orleans Parish (48 hours) vs. all other parishes (15 days), p. 57. But note that the parties can stipulate, in any parish, that the notary instead deliver the instrument to them or otherwise refrain from filing, relieving the notary of the duty, p. 58.

7. *Louisiana civil law tradition and organization of code law.* Ch. 2-5.

As with notarial practice, above, the legacy of general knowledge seems here to stay even if it's not emphasized in the SOS website. This may include: how the common law differs (e.g., civil law's supremacy of the legislature vs. judge-made law); structure of the court system; what "law" is just advisory (Attorney General opinions, and to some extent even court decisions); and origins of our civil code (especially its distinction from "Napoleonic Code"). They even test—maybe one question?—*where* in the statutes certain law will be found (e.g., notary law is in Title 35, small successions in the Code of Civil Procedure), which would be hard if you had not indexed subjects beyond what the glossary offers.

Besides the several introductory chapters, areas of substantive law later in the book (matrimonial regimes, lease, security agreements, corporate forms, etc.) seem ideal for several miscellaneous questions, but would be quickly answered if you'd indexed the study guide and can find the specifics. All tolled, such legacy questions and other standalone ones (devoted to specifics not tied to a scenario) may comprise 20-25 questions of about 80. You simply cannot skip reading the introductory chapters closely, and indexing areas of substantive law later in the book, even areas inapt for a scenario. Grab the miscellaneous low-hanging fruit.

8. *Power of attorney.* Ch. 15.

Although you must know the difference between procuration and mandate (the former is unilateral and is always in writing), in reality they are two flavors of the same instrument: *power of attorney*. This has nothing to do with attorneys as such, but instead delegates—from principal to agent—the power to act on behalf of the principal who makes it. The agent can be called an attorney-in-fact, because of their power to act legally or sign legal documents for someone else, but it's not the unauthorized practice of law. (Agent is also called a mandatary or representative, depending on whether it happens to come under a mandate or procuration.)

The document creating this relationship, using the common law term that the study guide makes clear is fine for these purposes, is the power of attorney (POA). It's used in simple business deals, as when a real estate agent acts on your behalf to make an offer, or when you authorize GEICO to sign your car title as part of the totaling of your wrecked car. Or it can be used in complex and emotional family issues (letting someone make medical decisions for you, then called a medical mandate or health care power of attorney), or more complex business decisions, as when all siblings delegate to one of them the power to deal with and eventually donate the family home they've inherited together. The POA is so commonly tested that you may want to write out a sample form in a blank place of the book, and index to it.

Louisiana POAs, unlike in many other states, are by default "durable" (p. 236), meaning the contract and the agent's power continue even if the principal gets incapacitated. (A principal in the original act can always make it non-durable.) Of course, one of the main reasons people execute a POA is to allow the agent to act in the event of a disability.

In the family situation, the main thing they test is the conditional procuration (p. 226), in which medical and business decisions are invested in the agent, but only *after* a condition of disability happens to the principal. Then you have to know not only how the original power of attorney is properly drafted, but also how to create an act that triggers the delegation—that declares the disability occurred. That has to be established following a specific process (with either one doctor or two certifying it, depending on how the original procuration is worded), and it's an authentic act.

Another testable subject, for POAs even without a condition to trigger it (most of them do take effect immediately), is the requirement that the agent's powers be specified and not generally stated. For the agent to be able to transfer land, the POA must say so (p. 229). The book stresses that the power to *donate* must be spelled out; just authorizing "transfers" doesn't empower donation (pp. 229-30). Similarly, a "general" POA that doesn't specify medical decisions isn't treated as a medical mandate.

Finally, they test whether a POA must be an authentic act. Technically, "no," so it can be informal (the mandate version, as a contract between two people, doesn't even have to be in writing, but it usually is for any serious transaction besides agreeing to buy a scratch-off together). *BUT* the agent's power to act is limited by the form of the original empowerment: they can only do what the POA instrument allows them to do. This is not just a rule, above, of what has to be specified in the POA, but also its *form* (p. 227). If not in writing, it doesn't allow the agent to do something that requires a writing, like taking out a mortgage. If not in authentic form, the agency is limited to doing acts that themselves don't require authentic form. For example, donation of immovables is an authentic act, so the POA empowering it must be authentic, too; same with a POA used to sign, second-hand, a mortgage using a confession-of-judgment clause.

For this reason, in practice many POAs are both authentic and specific, giving the agent broad authority. They may test you with a POA that would work just fine for a decision, like many medical ones, that don't have to be done via authentic act—but it fails as a device to allow the agent to do something listed among the many acts requiring authentic form (p. 295). This is especially testable because it requires you to know this rule about the form of POAs *and* which acts are authentic, making you look in two places of the guide.

A list of the things one cannot do via POA is in our ch. 15. Chief among them are making testaments and affidavits, since donating after death and swearing an oath are *personal* acts. This means that even a POA in authentic form purporting to delegate will-making to a relative doesn't actually permit that.

9. *Miscellaneous family law issues.* Ch. 12, 24, and 29.

They seem to pick one area of legal change to a family situation and ask a few questions about it within a section on another area of law, such as wills or property rights—if not in an entire section of its own. Examples ripe for testing include: limited emancipation; tutorship by will; temporary authority to make medical and educational decisions for a minor; acknowledgment of paternity; and adult adoption.

Most such contexts have a discussion about the law in one place in the book, then a form to accomplish it elsewhere (often in ch. 29), as with tutorship (pp. 168 and 539). The two places repeat a lot of the same information, but there may be some aspect that is on one page but not the other (such as recordation rules). Each subject is fully covered if you write page-specific cross-references (see our ch. 13, below, with detailed page references to insert into each place) or you index all places (ch. 12). Knowing just one of the two or three places where the issue is handled won't be enough on game day, as you can't count on one discussion being enough to answer their question. In fact, you should study the areas of non-overlap, because you can guess that's what they'll test.

10. *Property descriptions.* Ch. 22.

Though it makes sense to include this in the top-10, and the chapter must be read, it's a strategic question whether knowing it inside and out will pay off for the exam. There have been nightmare administrations in the early 2010s that featured several difficult questions (and had low pass rates), and some of the 2018 exams had multiple questions on the subject. Lately, for most exams, it seems to be a few miscellaneous questions if tested at all: July 2019 had practically none, other than recognizing what to do with property straddling parishes—more about filing; October had two or three questions at most, and they were more definitional and straightforward than difficult math examples of metes and bounds. Decoding every nuance of this chapter may take enormous time spent on other matters more testable and certainly more used in practice—it'd be malpractice for you to create a property description from scratch as part of a land transfer.

At the least, learn the actual examples the study guide gives, such as how to read a 36-square section, p. 367, and the kinds of questions they quiz on pp. 383-84. Know the "common mistake" they highlight at p. 379. And generally know the terms such as metes and bounds, p. 372, as opposed to describing by sections or by subdivisions, p. 377, the latter being easier—or the *per aversionem* form, p. 371, which was identified by its definition in an April 2019 question.

Most likely, they'd test descriptions in relation to other subjects, such as recordation—where the question looks like it's about the description but is answered by a different chapter in the book, wasting the time of someone stuck on ch. 22 on test day. If you can follow the sample quizzes in the study guide itself, even without knowing more difficult problems, you're probably ready.

Additional Testable Issues by Chapter

Within each chapter, or for each subject matter, there seem to be a few notable topics that are ripe for testing. This is simply my best estimate, based on: emphases in the study guide (look for rules or case law repeated in two or more places in the book, or for topics where it says something like "a good notary would know..."); information from last year's examinations; hints in the old exam questions at the end of other recent guides; topics that make for difficult but fair testing based on the author's test-writing experience; and suggestions made by experienced notary prep teachers observing exams the past few years.

It's not some "inside baseball" from the examiners themselves. Still, in each chapter, there has to be an emphasis on knowing cold these specific subtopics, or at least being able to find details about them during the exam. Here's a list of possibly emphasized topics for each chapter—by chapter number—but it's not meant to be to the exclusion of other topics.

The following is largely *in addition to* the topics already noted above in this chapter under other headings, such as the top issues by subject matter. The following, by chapter number, may not be in the top 10—or weren't covered above otherwise—but they deserve your attention.

1. notary as public official • importance of the authentic act and record-keeping

2. civil law judges only interpret the law • legislature is supreme law-maker

3. Louisiana notaries have more powers and responsibilities than common law ones • in this sense notaries are professionals and more than "official witnesses"

4. authority to revoke or suspend commission for cause rests with the courts • specifically the level of court most involved with such matters is the District Court, since that's where a rule to show cause would be filed by the DA or AG (p. 587).

5. general organization (books) of the Civil Code • meaning of "jurisprudence"

6. Clerk of Court is "parish recorder" • list of notarial instruments recorded with Clerk of Court (p. 40)

7. official misconduct, including misfeasance and malfeasance • injuring public records • notary's powers listed by R.S. 35:2 • duty to record • liability of notary

8. corporeal, incorporeal, movable, immovable • fruits • acquisitive prescription

9. usufruct: fruits, termination, divisibility, inventory • predial servitude: negative, affirmative, apparent, nonapparent • usufructary cannot create predial

10. list of prohibited donations (p. 129) • four exceptions to requirement of authentic act • acceptance: who, how, when • irrevocability and exceptions (split across pp. 124-25 and 140-42)

11. obligations is broader than contracts • types of contracts, list (p. 149) • four C's of contract formation • how "cause" is not "consideration" • nullity

12. domicile • tutorship • matrimonial regimes and agreements • fruits of SP=CP

13. things that may be sold, including a hope • ambiguities interpreted against seller • warranty of peaceful possession • lesion (only by seller, only if immovable)

14. lease requires: thing, rent, term • recording lease • transfer of ownership

15. list of termination of mandate (p. 232) • completion after principal dies

16. three kinds of suretyship • guarantor is not a joint debtor in true suretyship

17. two ways pledge still exists • largely replaced by UCC9 security agreements • perfection of a security interest

18. property that may be mortgaged • recording a mortgage • cancellation • documents as part of collateral mortgage package • recording collateral mortgages

19. see ch. 8, 9, and 11 below, discussing in detail the much-tested notarial acts

20. see ch. 7 below, on affidavits and verification of pleadings

21. vendor's lien or privilege • quitclaim deed • additional provisions for conveyances (p. 350) • content of mortgage • executory process • counterletters • NPI

22. forms of property description • finding a numbered section • describing one • following a metes and bounds description from commencing point • boundaries

23. odometer disclosure statements and when not required · affidavit of heirship · act of correction on certificate of title · sales and use tax · rescinded sales

24. see ch. 10 and 17, below, on notarial testaments, authentic form, separate property, and successions

25. creating trusts · who may be settlor, trustee, and beneficiary · recordation · use of trust principal for income beneficiary · forced portion in trust · refusals

26. reporting directly to court via certified copy of procès verbal · recapitulation is a summary

27. see ch. 10 and 17, below, on small successions (or succession-by-affidavit)

28. assumed business name (trade name) only applies to sole proprietorship, LLC, and partnership, not corp · articles of incorporation: content and filing

29. act of correction (two versions) · limits on "true copy" by notary, and certifying birth certificates · tutorship by will · act of partition · provisional custody by mandate

30. alternatives to personal appearance by all parties · confirmation of imperfect donation, to cure it · disclaimers, "attesting to signature only" · non-English acts

Common Mistakes to Avoid

Errors easily made but to be avoided by being aware and double-checking one-self:

1. *Definitional mix-ups.* One or two questions may actually turn on terminology trivia, such as remembering that "legatee," not "heir," fits with testate successions. I say "trivia" because in law practice it wouldn't matter much if you talked about an inheritor being an "heir" though really they take under a will. But on the exam...!

2. *Mixing up parties or roles in scenario.* They may use confusing names and relationships which are easy to blend under exam pressure. You may need to make a few notes in the scenario or library document to keep straight who's who. They may test parties not by actual names like Cathy but your understanding of role terms like mortgagee, legatee, and attorney in fact.

3. *Mixing up parties acting <u>in a role</u> in a scenario.* Meaning, they may be acting in a representative capacity rather than individually. It is no minor thing to keep straight which role they're acting in. Sometimes the same-named person acts for herself *and* in her role as agent, trustee, LLC member, or similar capacity, as for example "Martha" does in a sample scenario, p. 648. They're also big on knowing appearance clauses for people acting in such a capacity, splitting that across many places of ch. 19. Specifically, you can remember to name the principal first,

and all that appearance information in detail before introducing the agent (p. 298), by associating the word "principal" with "first": of *course* the principal goes first. You'll also be expected to figure out the proper signature line for such a person, e.g., "John Deaux, by and through his attorney in fact, Amber Dextris."

4. *Mixing up the "negative" of a question.* The format may ask which of the following statements is false (or ask what's true). It's easy in an exam situation to think you're answering correctly when that's the option they meant for you to *eliminate*. See p. 12 above about a method during the test to not trick yourself this way. Committing to marking the question up in this way may save a point or two just because the wording of the question is hard to follow or may be a double negative.

5. *Mixing up rules for intestate and testate successions.* For example, only intestate situations can (for in-state contexts) lead to a small succession procedure; only testate situations raise issues of forced heirship and disinheriting someone. (And the study guide mentions *twice*, pp. 423 and 450 that an olographic will can't provide for disposition of remains.) During the exam it's hard to keep the situations straight. Don't go only by memory; at least confirm any answer you're giving by locating it in the part of ch. 24 you should be on, for that scenario.

6. *Mixing up types of servitudes.* Usufruct is a *personal* servitude and is commonly tested. It's not the same as an encumbrance on the property itself because of the relationship between two tracts (*predial*), where you're focused on the dominant and servient estates (p. 106). Even within personal servitudes, there may be a question that sorts out usufruct vs. right of habitation vs. right of use (though usufruct is the most tested). These three are similar but you'll need to be able to find the key differences on exam day (such as that right of use is fully heritable and transferable, p. 105). And it's easy to confuse right of "passage" or "way" (p. 109), which is a predial servitude, with right of "use," which is personal. Indexing the terms may fix that.

7. *Counterintuitive words.* It's easy to test your (mis)understanding of definitions, as part of a larger question, when they words don't mean what they sound like. Look for these along the way and make a mental note that something's funky about the word. Examples: "private things" like cop cars can still be owned by the government, p. 80, not just "public things"; "vulgar" substitutions are actually OK, it's the regular ones that may be forbidden, pp. 130 and 437; and "legal" may mean done automatically by operation of law, not by a judge (a "judicial" act), so it's not the opposite of "illegal" (e.g., legal servitude, p. 108).

Also, "confusion" is a term of art for when the same person obtains both the dominant and servient estates (extinguishing the servitude, p. 120), and is sort of the opposite of "destination of the owner," p. 114. An "ordinary suretyship" is actually an uncommon form, p. 242. "Real right" is not really a right in real estate or real property, p. 248. The procès verbal is actually a written report, p. 485.

Some "donations" are not really acts of giving (more like contracts or repayments), so they aren't treated as donations and don't need authentic acts; some "sales" are such unfair exchanges, like a mansion for $1000, that it's not a sale but a "donation in disguise," pp. 133-34 and 569, needing authentic form (if not onerous or remunerative).

And, famously, naked owners may be fully clothed.

8. *Omitting formalities of or parties to an authentic act.* Many of the book's many "caveat notarius" warnings relate to a failure to use or formalize the required indicators of authentic form, such as order of signing, or actual presence of witnesses (e.g., pp. 561-65). It's such a recurring theme that they're signaling it'll be tested, and likely on more than one question.

Further common errors made in analyzing authentic acts are noted below at the end of ch. 8.

7

The Four A's of Notarial Functions

Chapter 19 of the study guide is the most important (if not the wills chapter, 24). It's dense, and worth reading several times. It is generally clear to follow, though there's some repetition and disorganization with topics that are introduced in a fairly lengthy way, then explained and illustrated more, later in the chapter. The most obvious culprit is the list of examples of phrases for "appearing" in various capacities (as an agent, as a member of an LLC, as a spouse, etc.). Pages 310-12 have many helpful examples—but then pages 301 and 321-22 have even more. Write cross-references in all three places within ch. 19 so that you'll know, on test day, to look in another spot for the example on-point to your question.

The main downside to chapter 19 is that it's so informatively dense, right from the start, that the authors never quite step back and explain why they break down various notarial acts the way they do, and how they relate to other important instruments covered in other chapters, like affidavits and wills.

The chapter below seeks to provide a bigger picture, to conceptualize the main functions of a notary. Our next chapter conceptualizes, and gives structure to, the *authentic act* in particular.

There are certainly more than four functions that notaries perform in Louisiana. Page 53 and the statutory appendix at page 582 spell out all the legitimate roles notaries play. The examiners do test that you recognize these broader functions, such as conducting family meetings, administering oaths (statewide, even for notaries with jurisdiction in limited parishes, as many have if commissioned before 2006), and managing inventories of estates (ch. 26). Notaries don't just do *four* things.

Still, the four *principal* functions, stated here in terms of the four main actions notaries perform, permeate the exam—and set up all the details of how they differ, readily tested (such as that many authentic acts can be done via an agent, while affidavits cannot). Your conceptual organization may vary and work fine, but I believe the easiest and most memorable way to organize most of what notaries do in practice—and what's most tested on the exam—is to think of these functions as *the four A's*. I've chosen an order to dispense with the two easiest functions first, both found outside ch. 19 of the study guide but related to the notarial acts detailed in that chapter.

1. ATTESTING TO SIGNATURES

The most basic function notaries perform is to identify a signer, watch them sign, and verify by the notary's seal (signature) that this person did sign this document. This works with forms that the notary has created and, often, with standardized forms the customer brings to the process. This attestation function is the one shared with common law notaries, who do have at least this very important role in commerce or public administration (if little else).

The main things tested about attestation are (1) the acceptable identifications or substitutes for ID allowed in the process of verifying who is signing (study guide pp. 71, 298), and (2) the ethical and practical necessity of making sure the right person signs, and does that in front of the notary. They may try to get you to regard some imperfect procedure as good enough, when it is not, such as the cautionary tale on p. 72 about having one signer vouch for the second signer's identity when neither signer is personally known to the notary.

These questions should be low-hanging fruit on the exam if you keep in mind that the easy way to comply is simply to do what you've sworn on the form that you've done: verify the person and watch them sign. They may also test whether the person is signing in the correct capacity (e.g., as an individual on one part of a form, but as an agent for another elsewhere on the form, as seen on a sample question at study guide p. 650). Finally, keep in mind that a mandatary or other agent signs their own name to the form, and is the one identified for attestation, rather than having the principal's named "forged" onto the signature line (below, p. 121).

2. AFFIDAVITS

Notaries administer oaths, as noted above, such as by swearing in a witness before a deposition or certifying an oath of office (as will be done for you when you take the oath before finalizing your commission with the SOS). One step beyond giving the oath is drafting and notarizing the affidavit, which is a fancy way of saying someone's written statement of fact made under oath.

It's conceptually accurate to see a properly drafted affidavit as similar to the framework and content of other notarial acts such as the authentic act. Many of the elements overlap, such as preamble, appearance clause, and conclusion. But the purpose and structure is just different enough, and easy enough to learn on its own, that it's best to see it as its own animal rather than a variation of other notarial acts like the authentic act. Nonetheless, at bottom the affidavit is an act—a unilateral juridical act (see p. 329)—with magic words such as the "jurat" (p. 540) that make it tick.

By "unilateral," the study guide simply means that it's not a group ritual the way authentic acts (and even contracts) are. It's just one person saying X is true, in front of a public officer swearing them in and verifying they read and signed it—swore to it in writing. It's so unilateral that the book emphasizes (p. 330) that the notary is not independently verifying the accuracy of the statements made by the affiant. Presumably it's perfectly all right for the notary to prepare and notarize a statement by the affiant that the affiant is divorced (which turns out not to be true) or drives a Mercedes (he in fact rides a Vespa). At the least there is no independent duty to investigate the facts sworn to, though there is some general duty of the notary to verify the competence of signers and actors in a transaction (see pp. 309-10 and 452).

By "juridical," the book simply means "legal" (i.e., relating to law or having legal consequences), not that it be done by a judge or in court. In fact, affidavits and many other juridical acts are often made out-of-court. Much of the point of affidavits and authenticated proof is to avoid having to establish the issue in a trial, if at all possible.

The *magic words* of an affidavit that certainly separate it from other notarial acts is the "jurat," meaning the phrase: "Sworn to and subscribed before me this ___ day of _____, 20_," and sometimes adding the city and state of signing (examples in study guide at pp. 330-31, and below, ch. 18). The term *jurat* may be tested, and certainly the requirement of the phrase is highly testable. A proper affidavit will have a jurat in its conclusion, while a different magic phrase is used for other acts, such as "Thus done and passed..." (p. 307). You know it's purporting to be an affidavit (or at least a variation like "verification of pleadings") when you see the jurat; and even some very different acts (such as a small succession affidavit) may also use such an attestation in closing.

The examples of affidavits given in the study guide are presented in the third person: the affiant as speaker but the notary as narrator. The affiant appears before the notary ("me") and swears to facts from the point of view of the memorializer of the statement, the notary, who repeats the statement in the third person ("that he is a resident of Caddo Parish"; "that she sold the car on July 23, 2017"; "that he was married but once, to Mary Smith").

In actual practice, affidavits may have the affiant tell her own story in the first person ("I am a resident of Caddo Parish," etc.). But one clear difference between an affidavit and a testament, for exam purposes, is that the testament is in the first person (the testator says "I") while the affidavit doesn't have to be, except for the introductory and conclusional contributions in the notary's voice. Remember that the notary is the one administering the oath, and the affiant's voice or content is contained within that shell. The formal parts are the notary's.

Even before the all-import closing lines (jurat with date, followed by signatures), the other distinctive feature of an affidavit is its "evidence of oath" before the core statements which the affiant is making. Here, you're expected to know that an affiant "appears" before the notary (perhaps in a briefer appearance clause than one would expect for an authentic act), who verifies that an oath was administered and the content is just about to follow. Typically the evidence of oath is the phrase: "Who, after being duly sworn, did depose and say...."

The exact structure and order of a valid affidavit it set out on p. 330 of the study guide. There, on the provided list near the top of the page, insert the requirement of a jurat ("Sworn to and subscribed before me...") between the bulleted lines on *the declaration* and *the date*, so as not to forget this is expected. I don't know why the book's "Components" list omits this crucial element, so handwrite it into the list. The jurat's phrasing *is* included on p. 331 and explained at p. 540.

You'll use it a lot in practice, even outside the context of formal affidavits (see p. 120 below).

Our ch. 18 has examples of actual affidavits, annotated. You may want to write this, or a similar complete sample of an affidavit, onto the blank part of the page opposite their components' list, so at study guide p. 331.

Also, somewhere near there, I *would've* advised writing a cross-reference to the affidavit's close cousin the "verification of pleadings." The table of contents says it's on p. 554, but it isn't (unless they reprint the book), or anywhere else in this edition. They forgot to include it from last year's. You may soon be able to see it on the SOS website and it may be included as an insert to future editions—if so, *write* it into the book and don't use it as a loose sheet. (This "fix" is my fault, sorry, because I told the notary division of their omissions—but not to get them to add more data, just to ask them not to test on it. I think they still could, so I explain it below anyway.)

In civil procedure nowadays, there's not as many uses for a verification of pleadings as there used to be, when all sorts of statements accompanying a lawsuit's filing had to be "verified" (notarized) and not just signed: procedure is streamlined now to make it less common. But for exam purposes you just need to know the notary's role in verifying pleadings, not the contexts that still require it. And in practice you will still get a regular number asking you to notarize a verification, so it ought to be included in the guide.

Whether they provide explanation to you or not, it's essentially an affidavit swearing that the pleading's assertions of fact are true (and a "verification of interrogatories" does the same thing for answers to discovery requests the other side in litigation has asked). The notary doesn't affirm their truth (just like with an affidavit), just that the signer affirms them. Verifying pleadings is not the practice of law—as would be drafting them or advising about them (p. 288).

By the way, here's the place to mention they also omitted the section on "subordination of mortgages," formerly also at the end of ch. 29 (along with part of a statutory form, though you can discern the rest of that). The concept is explained in the glossary, but there's no form to make one anymore unless they update the guide. If they do, write the form somewhere and index to it. Otherwise, at least know the definition they've left in.

3. "AUTHENTIC ACT" (INSTRUMENTS IN "AUTHENTIC FORM")

This is by far the most tested form of notarial instrument, especially when you consider that many other things they test on, such as donations and testaments, are forms of the authentic act. It is covered in ch. 19, as a general matter, and specific examples are found in many places throughout the study guide. You can create an index of all the acts that must be in authentic form by annotating p. 295, as suggested below, ch. 9. Our own list there expands on the entries already in your guide, and adds page references.

The concept and structure of the authentic act is our next chapter. The one after that shares all the instances in which authentic acts are required, followed by a chapter of some tips on the specific application of the notarial testament, which likewise must be in authentic form. Ch. 17 expands further on the concept behind wills and successions, allowing this difficult subject—which cuts across several chapters in the study guide—to be harnessed and answered on the exam.

4. ACKNOWLEDGED ACT

This is the poor stepchild of the authentic act. But it has some real uses in practice where not all the parties can come before a notary, or two competent witnesses are or were not present. It is covered below in ch. 11.

8

Concept and Structure of the Authentic Act

It's an Event, and You're Emcee and Narrator

Think of the authentic act as not just a document or legal instrument that accomplishes some goal. Think of it as an "act" in the sense of an *action*. It's an event. The document memorializes that event, but the event itself is important and has characteristics of its own, apart from the document produced from it. You know that a wedding is a ceremony, not just a bunch of signed forms. The authentic act isn't quite to that level of ritual and planning, but think of it along those lines, with the notary officiating.

The notary, in an authentic act, is not just an attester of signatures to a complex document. And not just a scribe to someone else's facts (as with the affidavit). Instead, the notary is the emcee to an event—a literal master of ceremonies. In the process the notary is also the narrator and memorializer of the event. The document that results is not so much a *product* of the event as it is a play-by-play *narration* of it. Once you understand that this is more than a signing ceremony (though it is that, too), all the ritual and formal requirements of an authentic act make sense. It is certainly a role for the civil law notary unlike anything found in the common law—where a notary would commit the unauthorized practice of law by acting as an active participant in (or even worse, emcee of) the legal procedure at hand.

Notaries in Louisiana cannot practice law, either (stressed at study guide pp. 74-76 and 499, and certainly testable). But many aspects of a notary's role in overseeing legal instruments are not *defined* here as the "practice of law," if a notary does it without giving legal advice. While in Kentucky or Kansas, say, creating a will for someone even without offering legal advice (just memorializing the wishes of the testator) could be a crime. So the same prohibition—don't "practice law" unless you're a lawyer—is true in all states. But Louisiana deviates greatly in allowing the notary a substantive, independent role in the authentic act.

Given that notaries here may officiate at authentic acts (oversee the event, draft the document), and that many types of legal actions can only be taken via authentic acts (see our next chapter), the notary exam heavily tests all aspects of this event and document. Understanding the concept of the act and the notary's emcee/narrator's role at the meeting that takes place makes it more intuitive to see how such acts are structured and how the ritual must be performed.

All authentic acts share a similar structure, that should be written somewhere accessible in the book. The guide shows the structure for an affidavit on p. 330, but somehow omits a similar bullet-point for the more-tested authentic act (the list on p. 296 is too generic, for "juridical acts"). I set it out below, in bold, with some explanatory notes, unbolded, you could write in, or shorten. The best place to write it is on the last blank page of the guide (facing the inside back cover), leaving room to add all sorts of notes, phrasings, examples you'd like to have handy as you construct such an act. Use page numbers to make the framework a mini-index, too. Our ch. 18 offers an example of an authentic act, annotated.

The structure below makes sense if you think of the authentic act as a *story* told by the notary about an event. After the title, and setting of location (venue), the notary introduces himself or herself (introduction), then welcomes in the key players (appearances), describes the main action of the plot (body of act), then winds up the tale (conclusion). Once everybody signs off it in the proper order, the script is done.

Thinking of it as a story with characters who appear at different times also helps you to remember the order in which they must sign, which is testable (and should be written somewhere handy as a reminder, such as top of the AA page, 295; see next chapter). The *order of signing* is always:

parties → 2 witnesses → notary

Drafting Authentic Acts and Structure: Write into Study Guide

- **Title** (Heading), e.g., "Act of Correction" or "Limited Emancipation by Authentic Act"

- **Venue** (or can precede Heading): "it's where your feet are" is the catchy reminder by Shane Milazzo

- **Introduction** (Preamble): establishes the capacity of the notary

- **Appearance Clause(s)**: important *and testable* introduction of the parties to the act

- **"Body of Act"** (core): the law provides the defining *substance or content* of the act

- **Conclusion** (starts "Thus done and passed..."): ties it together

- **Signatures** (note recent statutory requirements: names under signing, notary ID #)

Common Mistakes with the Authentic Act

- Incomplete appearances, such as domicile (not residence) and neglecting the statutory requirement of change in marital status (not just marital history), including even a "no change" status

- Capacities and disqualifications, such as that the witnesses not have an interest in the act

- Forgetting the formal requirements of an authentic act, especially two witnesses

- Neglecting statutory requirements, such as the full names of all parties, witnesses, and notary placed beneath the signature (the latter easy to forget when so many of the sample forms in the guide, especially in chapters 19 and 30, inexplicably have a signature line drawn but don't add "printed or typed name" under the line, to remind you)

- Forgetting that a certain document must be in authentic form (or thinking one has to that doesn't, like a trust *inter vivos*, or act of sale), which is the next chapter

9

"AA": Acts Required to Be Authentic Acts
or in Authentic Form

Every course of study emphasizes how crucial the study guide's p. 295 is. All the acts and instruments that must be in "authentic form" (and not just "authenti-cated," as discussed below in ch. 11) are spelled out. If you tab or color-edge the book at all, it's probably to make it easy to reach *that* page in a flash. At some point that's unnecessary, because it's the one page (well, two, since it now spills over a line onto p. 296) you come back to so often in your study that you'll have no problem finding it exam day. Anyway, you *will* use it the day of the test.

The magic page can become even more functional if it's annotated by hand with page numbers, so that it serves as a mini-index to these authentic acts (shown below in bold).

It's not exactly true that they included *all* authentic acts on the page. You'll find it helpful to write in the extra situations, or contexts more specific than the magic page says, that use authentic acts or are in authentic form. They are set out below in bold, adding page references.

It is also important that, at every place in the book where an act is discussed that must be in authentic form, you mark it in a way that you can't miss, during the exam, the reminder that this event must be done authentically. I don't think highlighting "authentic form" or the like in the text is enough. It's best to use some unique, loud note at each place where authentic form is required, and one such way is explained here:

I've provided an expanded list, with pagination. It's best not to copy it mindless-ly, but engage it and follow the cross-references to find the place where that page says "authentic"—then *write AA in the margin at each spot*, possibly in your thickest marker or its own color. Every time you get to that act or situation in the book during the exam, you'll be reminded by the bold AA that this will need two witnesses and follow all statutory formalities like a full name (p. 298) and the names written or printed below the signature (p. 308).

Why is it so crucial to have a list handy of authentic acts and to annotate each place in the guide where they say it's required to be that? Because it's so tested. They are not likely to ask it in the form of "which of the following must be authentic acts?" But there will be someplace (or more) on the exam where they show a form that's missing some essential element of an authentic act, such as witness signatures. It's only "missing" if the act is authentic. Or they'll ask which people have to sign a document (as they do in the sample exam question, p. 649), and you have to name the witnesses and notary as part of the list they give.

Or the exam can have a list of acts in a question and ask which one is invalid if ... [showing an example that does not conform to authentic requirements]. So, the answer is the one that has to be an authentic act. A good decoy answer is one that often *is* in authentic form, but doesn't have to be, such as a document creating a trust *inter vivos* (p. 464 specifies that it could also be accomplished by a form of witness acknowedgment). In these decoy situations, where authentic acts are sufficient but not required, it's important that you *not* write "AA" there or highlight the "authentic" in the text, as it may catch your eye during the exam and trick you into assuming that it *needs* to be authentic. Instead, consider a different note to yourself (because these situations are so testable and counter-intuitive); for example, you could use bold, thick initials in the margin and explain it there in smaller print: ***AAAA***: ALLOWS ALTERNATE TO AA (or: acceptable alternative to AA).

Speaking of counterintuitive, it may help to conceptualize when AA is essential—explaining most of the magic page—in order to develop an intuition that seems second-hand during the exam (still, quickly check the open book to confirm your instinct when actually answering the question). I learned this organizing princi-ple from a PassMyNotary workbook, and it helped me, so I adapt and expand on it here. By instinct, ask yourself: what situations in real life *ought to* require the maximum formality and seriousness, and be witnessed in front of a notary by two responsible ("competent") undersigning people?

The answer makes sense if you imagine *two sets of life issues* where you wouldn't trust anything less than serious procedure and having witnesses. Two types of things the main signer is trying to accomplish where, cynically, it's awfully tempting to fake your identity or pretend someone else is OK with the result.

One set is situations in which family-shattering changes will result. Giving up children, adopting them, and even allowing people to make parental-type situ-ations are the epitome of fundamental family change. One shouldn't be allowed paternity of your kid without following the letter of the law. If it's not going to be done in court, and we allow it to be done privately, at least we should make sure you're who you say you are. And add a solemnity that confirms you're really sure you want to give up, say, parenthood of a child that is biologically yours. Even naming someone as a tutor (guardian) is a serious thing and ought to have for-malities to make it so.

A second set is situations in which property is immediately and permanently transferred, such as a donation that is totally one-way and not some kind of swap or repayment (contrast *onerous* and *remunerative* donations at pp. 126-27, the difference almost certainly tested). We simply cannot assume that some-one meant to do such a gratuitous gift if they are not physically there to sign the instrument making that happen. Imagine if Bob shows up in your notary office with a letter from Jane purporting to give Bob her hunting camp in St. Francisville. Bob is definitely Bob and is willing to sign it. But *of course* he is: he's *getting* the camp. If you could notarize that validly and it effectively transferred the camp just by Bob signing, the camp becomes Bob's without any real proof that this is what *Jane* wanted. And she'd have to hope Bob will give it back to her, because the transfer is immediate and *done*. Good luck with that!

As you can see, we don't allow such transfers on the say-so of the recipient/beneficiary who stands to gain, or even on the written instruction of the giver or seller. Even if the giver's letter is notarized or a proper affidavit. The lack of two witnesses and solemn ritual makes even the confirmed giver's letter insufficient to create such a huge property-altering result.

That's true even if property is transferred only at your death: it's a serious thing and fraud is so tempting if it's not clear that the person designating who gets what (and who's cut out) is the actual testator. So even testaments by notary must be done in authentic form, even if it's not the typical AA and has its own structure and rules (like signature at bottom of each page), as exampled on pp. 460-62 of the study guide and discussed in our next chapter.

Oddly, an olographic (handwritten) will is not made in authentic form, so it's an AAAA. The test-makers will be very clear when they talk about a testament that it's a notarial one, or the library for the scenario is clearly a notary's version, not handwritten. And they are unlikely to ask much if anything about olographic wills (since by definition a notary is not involved), except perhaps to test the will-fail at pp. 560-61 where someone tried to hybridize the notary type with the olographic one—the notarized date did not substitute for the required testator-written one. Btw, in other states it's "holographic," like Notorious B.I.G.

In short, legal actions that have monumental importance (e.g., declaring you disabled from making choices about your own life) or invoke healthy skepticism (like someone just giving away a property out of love, to the immediate exclusion of the giver and other people who may want it) tend to require that, if they be done through a notary, they be authentic in every sense of the word.

Anyway, when you study the magic page 295 and its legendary list of AA-required documents, keep in mind the two sets of situations where it just makes sense that, short of a court order, the result will not happen without the most serious of notarial acts. The most serious ritual and double-verification we use in Louisiana, outside of court, is the authentic act.

Here's a way to make page 295 (and 296 top) even more magical: make it more complete, and cross-reference it to page numbers in the study guide where the act is detailed.

ACTS REQUIRED TO BE IN AUTHENTIC FORM

Adapted and expanded from C. Alan Jennings et al., *Fundamentals of Louisiana Notary Law and Practice* (2020 edition), pp. 295-96. Text in **bold** adds items or clarifications not found in the study guide's list at that page, as well as page numbers of the study guide for cross-referencing, if any (we list the first page of the topic only, not the entire page-range, when it's clear it continues). The page numbers and the extra entries can be written directly into the guide, as between lines in the list.

Note required signing order for all authentic acts: parties → witnesses → notary

The following acts or instruments must be *authentic acts* (**"AA"**) per Civil Code art. 1833 in order to be valid **(are absolutely null if not AA or in "authentic form")**:

- act of surrender (adoption) (Children's Code art. 1122)

- release of claims by alleged father; consent to adoption (Children's Code art. 1196)

- consent of parent to the adoption of child in an intrafamily adoption (Children's Code art. 1244)

- acknowledgment of paternity (C.C. arts. 190.1, 196; R.S. 40:34.5.2), **including 3-party form, 163, 524**

- **revocation of acknowledgment of paternity, 525**

- adult adoption (C.C. art. 213), **165, 528**

- **provisional custody by mandate: effectively AA when using statutory forms (of R.S. 9:954, 962), 554**

- designation of tutor ("tutorship by will," **or done inter vivos**) (C.C. art. 257), **169, 539**

- limited emancipation by authentic act (C.C. art. 368), **170, 540**

- modification or termination of limited emancipation by authentic act (C.C. art. 371), **171, 541**

- **a would-be beneficiary's *refusal* of interest in the trust (only if inter vivos) (R.S. 9:1985), 478**

- declaration of dispensation from collation (C.C. art. 1232), **see next**

- proof of conditions of partnership to exempt from collation (C.C. art. 1247), **508 (partnership contract)**

- **transfer (gratuitous) of Separate Prop → Community Prop must be AA, like donations, 183 (this even applies to movables)**

- donations inter vivos of immovables and incorporeal things (and corporeal movables whenever not effected by actual delivery or when the donation must be in writing) (C.C. arts. 1531, 1533), **134 ... But not remunerative** donations nor onerous donations (the latter just in writing, if immovable), unless donation in disguise so not truly remunerative or onerous, 127, 134

• donative transfer of a motor vehicle *title* is included in the above (must be AA to have OMV accept it), though transfer of actual ownership may be done by manual gift, 395

• most *confirmations* after-the-fact of donations inter vivos must be AA, 136, 565

• notarial testaments (C.C. arts. 1577-1580.1), **423**

• revocation of entire testaments(s) by testator (C.C. arts. 1607) ... Will can also be revoked by a new will, either notarial or olographic, and by other means, 440

• notarial codicils, 458

• act of mortgage or privilege on immovable property importing *confession of judgment* in order to use *executory process* (C.C.P. arts. 2631, 2635), **355**

• act of immobilization of a movable (R.S. 9:1149.4), **83**

• act to establish disability of principal in conditional procuration (R.S. 9:3890), **226; more on POA below**

• grant of real right in immovable created for educational, charitable, or historic purposes (R.S. 9:1252)

• act of sale of titled movable sold by holder of privilege (R.S. 9:4502)

• acknowledgement of designation of keeper of property (R.S. 9:5136)

• affidavit of correction (R.S. 35:2.1) (= "act of correction"), by notary or by parties, 527, 583 ... But compare act of correction for error on a *vehicle* title: need not be AA, 400

• affidavit of distinction, if using the optional statutory form of R.S. 9:5501.1, is effectively AA, 531

• act to cancel mortgage or privilege secured by paraphed obligation (R.S. 9:5170), **270**

• statement of authority, **used for unincorporated associations** (R.S. 12:505), **358, 523**

• any procuration or mandate (POA) must be AA, to be effective *if* the power it's authorizing (like donation) itself requires AA; need not be AA if power doesn't require AA ... So, for agent to execute a document required to be AA, the original POA must be AA, 227

• But 4 things cannot be done by POA: will, affidavit, marriage, adult adoption [a list we also note in ch. 15, below]

10

Notarial Testaments and Successions

The "testament," a/k/a "will," is simply a donation made upon death (*mortis causa*). Like donations made while still living (*inter vivos*), it must be an authentic act when done by a notary—when not "olographic."

The same concept of an authentic act applies to the notarial testament, and it must be in authentic form. So the outline structure given earlier for other such acts generally applies to wills, too—with minor variations in the kind of appearance clause used (for example, it sets out residential address instead of domicile), and a major difference in the attestation clause's exact language you are expected to use for a will.

But it's different enough overall—and an excellent, annotated example is in the study guide at pp. 460-62—that, to answer questions, you can use the book's own exemplar instead of your notes about other authentic acts.

Still, keep in mind the related *idea*, the shared sense that they are all events which the notary emcees and doesn't just attest to. Much the same warnings apply: if you remember it's an action and not just a paper, it makes sense to have the witnesses see the testator sign it, and in an exact order (pp. 559-60); it makes sense that special rules apply for testators who are impaired in some way (p. 424); and it makes sense that witnesses to a will be more "competent" and less conflicted (pp. 316-18) than they have to be in other settings.

All such acts use magic words at very specific places in the document (just as the jurat is the magic for an affidavit), though the words change for this different context: donating property upon death. Its own special catchphrases, such as the attestation clause dictated by statute, are routinely tested.

To the extent it is not clear from the book's annotated example, here is the structure of the typical testament:

- venue
- title
- appearance
- dispositive portion
- testator signature after that (and on each page)
- date
- attestation clause

- two witnesses' signatures
- notary's signature

Having an author-approved exemplar of a valid will makes it easy if they do ask a question that tests your understanding of the rules and terms. Most likely the question would draw on some clarification in the sample's footnote annotations, such as the difference between a *universal* legacy and a *particular* one (also called specific legacy). They certainly may test your remembering that each page before the signature page also has the testator's signature at the bottom. So, go ahead and draw a big star next to the name-lines on these pages. And draw arrows to make them go where they're *supposed* to go, from the tops of the guide's pages to the bottom of the page before (somehow in revising this edition, the editors erroneously moved them from the legally correct spot—the *bottom*).

But since the good example is there and easy to locate, it's more likely they will give you an *imperfect* example in your test library and make you explain (in multiple choice) why it's invalid, or figure out ways to make it valid. Some features of the will they provide may look menacing, such as that the notary is named as an executor as well, leading you to look elsewhere in the chapter to be sure that's allowed (it's OK, see p. 435).

The library's sample testament may also be written in the third person, sounding more like an affidavit than the sample in the guide does (which says "I" for the testator). By itself that's not a problem as long as the core, dispositive portion is written in the first person. An example of a valid will that does have some third-person POV to it is shown below in ch. 18, just so you wouldn't be thrown off too much by the change in perspective from the exemplar in the guide. A will's not an affidavit, and not written using a jurat, but it can be *introduced* in the third person the way other acts are.

Ultimately, though, it's a statement of the testator's intent, not the notary's or anyone else's. And it is a *singular* event, not only in the sense of "important," but also meaning two people can't join to make one testament (p. 421). That's unlike many acts, and even some affidavits like the small succession one of ch. 27, which contemplates a group verification of assets and agreement—it can't be signed by just one person, in fact (p. 497).

The examiners often combine a will (or will library) with other substantive issues that make you look beyond ch. 24 for an answer to the specific question asked. They often create a trust in the will (ch. 25), or ask questions about the succession that follows, or test on the usufruct as a byproduct of the will (or of intestate inheritance). Sometimes a whole section of the exam entitled "testament" may be less about the will as such as it is used as a steppingstone to test understanding of community property ownership and transfer, donations, family relations such as emancipation or tutorship, and trust law.

As for successions, they often test the small succession procedure (often called now "succession by affidavit," since there are some instances where even large estates worth more than $125,000 can take advantage of it). They use successions to test your understanding of usufruct and community property, for example that the estate of the deceased technically doesn't include the surviving spouse's share of the community. With such scenarios they often make you do math, believe it or not, for instance to determine whether the remaining estate qualifies as a small succession (see ch. 17 below).

Successions without a valid will are "intestate"—and they often test the term for that, as well as "heirs" (intestate donees) versus "legatees" (receive by testacy, i.e., in a will). No notary is involved in intestate succession (unless one wrote an invalid will that fails, so it's *the same as* "intestate"—a plausible situation to get tested). So you may think they wouldn't ask about it. But the rules of succession are the kind of general Louisiana property law they expect you to learn well, or at least index well and be able to answer the day of the exam. Particularly because intestate inheritance affects several aspects of testate succession.

One instance when the testate/intestate rules formally overlap, and become testable, is when the percentage of an estate must be left to a child through forced heirship regardless of the testator's intent. The percentage—more math—may be a function of the number of forced heirs and the default they would get if the decedent had no will (explained below, pp. 103-05). So, you have to know intestate succession, which itself doesn't have forced heirship, even in a testate succession where forced legacies are involved with at least one child surviving.

Finally, they often test other rules of forced heirship. Two big subjects: (1) a forced heir can be 24+ if they are disabled at the time of decedent's passing, including situations like bipolarism more subtle than a wheelchair (p. 436), and (2) the grounds for disinheriting a forced heir are limited and statutory (pp. 445-46); for exam purposes, they're non-negotiable and you can't go off the list to name one that doesn't fit the accepted situations allowing disinherison. If it's not literally on the list, the answer is: the legacy is forced.

The subject of testaments, successions, and community property law is pervasive and difficult, but the study guide never quite presents the big picture. The details are there, and can be indexed by subtopic, yet most students also need a way to wrap their heads around the whole. Our ch. 17 attempts to visualize the concept for you. Now's the time to turn to the final "Notarial A," but if you have difficulty with wills and related subjects, the additional chapter on property and wills may be helpful.

11

Acknowledged Acts

The full name is "acts under private signature duly acknowledged," and that indicates the actual process used: private acts turned into something more by coming to a notary. But it's fine to call them *acknowledged acts*. They may also be called "authenticated acts," though that's too close to "authentic acts" to keep straight, so it's best not to use the term. The latter term does capture the notion that such instruments are self-proving in court—they are technically "authenticated" for purposes of admission into evidence without having to use a witness at trial to verify they're real.

That self-proving quality of acknowledged acts is shared with the full-blown authentic act. Both self-prove (study guide p. 289), which is important in how the document is used at law. But for notary exam purposes, it's likely that the examiners focus more on the main difference between the two acts: where a situation calls for an authentic act (see above, ch. 9).

The authentic act is perhaps more pervasively tested on the notary exam because it comes up in more notarial contexts than do acknowledged ones. Still, a question or two on acknowledged acts is predictable because it forces you to sort through two wholly different versions of such acts, as discussed in the study guide at pp. 290-92 and summarized below.

So, the two most likely key points to be tested: (1) these two different options for acknowledging a private act, easily muddled, and (2) the relatively few situations in which an acknowledged act works as a fair substitute for the authentic act, or even is required for a document if not truly authentic.

The best example of number 2 is an instrument creating a trust *inter vivos* (p. 464). I suggested in ch. 9 that when you see such examples in the study guide, boldly mark AAAA in the margin to remind you on game day that it's not on the magic list of acts requiring authentic act (p. 295). In most such situations, the law requires *either* an authentic act *or* an acknowledged one.

A harder question, because it is not just a matter of scavengering the answer from the margin of your guide, would test your understanding of my number 1 above: the two different ways, using two different statutory bases, a notary can authenticate a private act signed outside the presence of the notary. Even though the answer might be figured out by applying p. 290 of the guide, that snippet is a bit confusing, so a big picture and example may make it clearer.

To step back a bit: both situations involve something signed outside the notary's presence (earlier in time) and both involve two witnesses; the key difference is *when* those witnesses get involved. Almost by definition, both contexts fail to have both parties to the transaction before the notary, since then it could easily be done by authentic act simply by having it witnessed there. So the context for an acknowledged act nearly always is one where the notary has only *one* of the two parties in their office. The two contexts both fill a need to have the document be more than just signed even if it is less than authentic. They both scratch an itch for something to be self-proving even if it amounts to "authentic-light."

Picture two parties in an IHOP who agree to a deal, scrawl out the terms on a napkin, and both sign it. What if they want it to be more than just a private act, to be something that holds up in court without having to haul the parties there to introduce the contract into evidence? But one can't make it to your office? The law gives them two great options short of the authentic act, both requiring a notary and two witnesses. They differ mainly in *when* the witnesses do their job. (Btw, if the problem is just that they both can't show up together, they could still do it as an authentic act by each executing it separately before different notaries—or the same notary at different times—just as many documents are executed separately but combine to be treated as one, pp. 558-59. We'll ignore this shortcut here, because that result is simply "authentic" if done right.)

If two people watching in IHOP served as witnesses, that's half the battle. But without witnesses then and there, you'll need two at the notary's office. Either option of authenticating a private act needs two witnesses *at some point*. The two methods, with two statutory sources, are:

Acknowledgment by party (C.C. art. 1836)

After an act under private signature was made, one party goes to the notary and acknowledges it, recognizing the prior signature as his or her own in front of two [new] witnesses. This way doesn't necessarily have to be witnessed when it was originally signed.

So the IHOP-deal made with no witnesses at the scene can still be authenticated, after the fact, by having either party confirm it in front of the notary and two witnesses, as long as the notary collects those signatures in the proper order as with an authentic act (party, witnesses, then notary) and as long as the requirements of Title 35 are met (e.g., the witnesses' names below the signatures). The procedure to do this is in the form of an acknowledgment of an existing document.

Acknowledgment by affidavit of prior witness, grantor, or vendor (R.S. 13:3720)

After an act under private signature was made, and properly witnessed *at the time* with two witnesses, the instrument can be acknowledged by an affidavit (before a notary) made either: (1) by the vendor or grantor swearing he did sign it in front of the witnesses, or, most usefully, (2) by one or both of the [original] witnesses setting forth that the instrument had been executed before them. In the latter version, a party essentially drags a witness to the notary with him and makes the instrument more official than it would otherwise be.

At the IHOP, where witnesses saw the parties sign the napkin, one (or both, but why?) can go with a party and execute the affidavit (and theoretically could go without a party). Or the party—if it's the one giving away the interest—can go without either of the prior witnesses but swear to the witnessed napkin signing before. Why the one giving the interest? We're more skeptical of the *recipient* of property or an interest; the one who's giving it away is less likely to be doing it fraudulently. In our IHOP example, if it's a valid and mutual exchange, either party could be considered a grantor or vendor. If they test this option, my guess is they would make it clearly a vendor (seller), or make it clearly the opposite party (buyer) so this option is not available—but then that party could use the other option, requiring two *new* witnesses.

They may also test this option by relating it to a more general rule about affidavits: these are personal to the affiant, and cannot be delegated to an agent or mandatary. The procedure to do this option is in the form of an affidavit about a previous event—the signing—and an existing document. It would be a wrong answer to have someone else claim to be acting on behalf of the party, even with all the paperwork to show they have that mandate (a power of attorney to act for the party), since this option is an affidavit.

Similarly, an affidavit not made before a notary cannot be made valid by witness acknowledgment (p. 291).

A third form? Car title transfers (and a note on vehicle donations)

Although it's not presented in chapter 19 on acknowledgments, in reality there's another situation where a witness matters after-the-fact much like the "affidavit of prior witness" version just above. That's when a vehicle buyer and seller want to transfer title but they aren't both going to the notary, found in ch. 23.

The usual way is for buyer and seller to show up to the notary and sign ("endorse") the certificate of title (often also with a bill of sale, p. 395, though it's not required). Even just the seller signing in front of a notary will do (p. 388). But otherwise, the back of the certificate allows the transfer, even when not signed before a notary, by having it signed by the seller, as witnessed by two witnesses who also sign at the time (in the left column). Then one of the witnesses goes to the notary and acknowledges the prior signing, here in the longer text below the columns. The notary verifies the witness's signing there. A textual version of this process is also laid out on p. 388.

This is a useful process, much like the R.S. 13:3720 one for various documents, in situations where it's anticipated that one party (usually, seller) is finished with the transaction by signing at someone's home or a car lot, with no notary handy. The OMV still regards the certificate and vehicle as transferred.

During the exam, despite the different context, you can consult the form on p. 388, and its acknowledgment clause ("a witness to the signature(s) of seller(s)"), for language that illustrates how witness acknowledgment works generally.

A sample bill of sale is provided below, in our ch. 18. An act of donation would be used to transfer a car, boat, trailer, etc. without compensation. This usually needs to be an authentic act, and with written acceptance by the donee, for OMV to issue a new certificate of title—as the study guide emphasizes in a new part of the 2020 edition, and thus very possibly tested, at p. 395.

By the way, and unrelated to using witnesses to fill the gap, the absent party could also empower someone to go to the notary *for* him or her, by using a power of attorney. Often that's done, for example, when there are two owners listed on the front page, but one is going to take the lead in the sales process.

12

Index and Additional Definitions

Your own hand-inserted index need not be as exhaustive or duplicative as the below. It just needs to lead you to the right parts of the book during the exam, and deal with the fact that the relevant information is often spread across two or more places in the book. Still, my goal is to make it usable during the time-limited and nerve-wracking test. To that end, I don't follow every norm of indexing—such as efficiency of having only one entry for an idea—because users need to find the page references fast, in the first place they look (e.g., including both "pet trust" and "animal trust"; or both "surviving spouse" and "spouse, surviving"). So, repeating information fully in two or more places may save time.

There's also limited room in the glossary, so I use some abbreviations (you'll likely use more, or shorter ones), and I state things very briefly—just enough to point you to the guide's discussions. I don't tend to cross-reference with words only (like "will—see testament"), instead writing the same page numbers in both places. I break three other norms of indexing, though you don't have to, as you write it into the guide.

First, it's not perfect alphabetical order (oddly, neither is their glossary). Items have to be inserted where there's space between glossary words. That doesn't always happen in perfect order. I'm not worried you'll miss spying an entry that's a few words away from where it should be; I *am* worried you won't fit it all in if you ignore open space just to stay in line. I try to keep order, sure, but you'll see the below is often fitted to where there's room to write.

Second, true indexes name the range of pages for a topic (like "pp. 61-62"), but I usually list the first page only. It's enough to get you to where the topic starts, and you'll readily see the conversation continues to the next page. Only where the range of pages is more than a few pages, so you might miss the globality of the topic, do I use ranges. There's a whole section on predial servitudes, so I cover the whole, for instance.

Third, I don't always list the page numbers in ascending order. Where there's a page you clearly should find first, I put it first ("348, 40, 600"). I don't want to skip any page that mentions the topic, but often there's a key place to look and some related pages. They do test your ability in one question to put together information from two places in the book, so all listed pages are potentially useful. But some are more on-point or thorough than others. This artifice is truly optional since it may confuse some who'd prefer to re-right the page order; just do so as you copy it. But I think you want prioritization and not just "any mentions." I'm hoping the first place you look answers the question. Or that in reviewing, you see at a glance the first page you should read. (You could also right the order but underline the most important number.)

Note that I put in **bold**, below, any terms that are already in the glossary. This isn't meant to emphasize them, just to indicate it's already there and you only need to insert page numbers or a few added thoughts (not in bold). I use many subentries (sorted by semi-colons, or new lines with hyphens) where thoughts are broken down more. Parsing concepts is a valuable indexing norm that helps the day of the exam.

The following expanded, annotated index is meant to be hand-copied right into the existing glossary, of course, but it's best not to make it only a mindless copying task. Sure, the first round of that can be done in front of the TV or while watching a child's swim practice. At some point you need to *engage* the index and follow the main points to their specific page, especially the first page mentioned that is most instructive. You should see this index as a dialog and aid to the studying process, not just as a list to copy.

I noted earlier (ch. 9) that just adding page numbers to the magic-AA-page is not as effective as also using it to go write "AA" boldly at the source text. Here, too, it's best to use the index to go find the main point assigned and to be familiar with the related material around it. It's about effective studying, not just open-book test-taking. Yet even copying it for exam day will make a few extra questions, and probably even more than a few, answerable under the pressure and time limits they impose.

At this point, we'd like to add that this annotated index is one of the most important parts of this book. It'd be easy to copy and share it. We'd appreciate it if you'd respect the copyright of this work and not do that. We tried to price the book low so that anyone who wanted any part of it could buy it (or even cheaper eBook versions). The hope is that users will share their awareness of this index with others—and share their views, pro or con, about it and the tips in this book—without just sharing the index alone. (And I'd like to justify the effort to update it every year, when a new guide comes out, besides assigning it to my students.) Thanks for considering that reality.

INDEX AND ADDITIONAL EXPLANATIONS

Notes:

- **bold** = already a glossary entry; bold *isn't* used here to mean emphasis
- some glossary terms, bold, don't have a page number if the entry suffices
- -- means a subentry; this is also done on one line divided by semi-colons
- commas before page numbers usually omitted unless unclear otherwise
- page number listed is often the first page of discussion; few page *ranges*
- alphabetical order is deviated from when there's more space, nearby, to insert new entry into existing glossary
- page numbers may not be in ascending order; first entry is most useful
- some abbreviations or short statements are used here; you can use more

-- form to Appear 311

-- attaching corp doc to act, 325

corporeals 81

counter letter 359

correction, affid of (act of), 527-28, 583

-- by notary 527 (clerical error only; is AA)

-- by party 528 (also AA)

-- for car/vehicle title 400 (not AA)

covenant marriage 176

credit deed

credit sale 334

cum onere 265; clause 350

custodian of private docs (re discovery) 538

custodian: nonlegal custd'n affid 543 (med or educ consent)

curator / curatrix 173

corrupt influencing 45, 47 (related to bribery)

date on will 453; failure of olographic 560

dation en paiement 128, 344

declaration of life-sustaining procedures 316

declaration of acquis of sep prop 182

decedent 406

de facto doctrine 67

degree 409 (re successors)

de jure 67

dereliction 86 (like alluvion)

derogation, acts in 288, 150 (null); contracts 155

designate tutorship 539

destination 114

descendants 408 (direct lineage, down)

disability, act establish'g 226 (AA; re procuration)

disclaimers 307, 577 ("notary not prepared this")

disclosures at closing 360

dishonor

discovery 538

'discussion of assets' 504

disguised donation 133, 568

disinherison 444-47; form to 436-37

dissolution of donation 142

distinction, affid of 529

disposable portion 435

dollar: 'one dollar & consideration' 569

domicile 300, 161 (≠residence, 300)

-- sworn intent to change 539

donation inter vivos, ch 10; form & content 347-50

-- AA usually, but exceptions: 134

-- d in disguise 133, 568

-- d of titled movable 395

-- null d, 128; cure for 136, 565-67 (confirm imperfect d)

-- d of future prop is null 348

-- d of naked ownership? prob not, 124

-- ways to accept d of immov 137, 349

-- *who* can accept d 138

13

Cross-referencing Expanded, and by Page Numbers

The study guide has a lot of cross-references built into it. That's good because it often splits information about one topic over two or more places. There's no real reason why they should detail limited emancipation on pp. 170-72 and then provide the form to do it on p. 540. On the day of the exam you may need to consult both places, or more, to answer a question. That's especially so if my suspicion is correct that they create many questions with the goal of making you look in both to figure out the answer. Even a straightforward question can have their desired level of difficulty if the answer combines parts of the book from different chapters, so you wouldn't get it right glancing at the table of contents.

To that end, using cross-references in the text to other subject-matter locations is nearly as important as annotating an index. At least the book already uses cross-references, and you may be able to get by with them as-is. There are two ways to improve it: First, use more cross-references than they already have. I offer a few that seem to be missing in some testable areas, further below. You could add more as you study. And you may well use them on test day; you can also quickly check the index entry for that subject to see if it lists two or more pages to check.

Second, paginate the cross-references. The way the book has them, they take you to a topic's chapter and heading, which is pretty useful but doesn't pinpoint the actual page. During the exam you may not easily find the heading. Even if you do, the answer may hide on one of the pages of that subject that isn't the page with the heading. It's better to use page numbers. Add them near the existing heading-based cross-reference, in both places (back to each other).

We expand cross-references both ways, below. We don't add cross-references to matter repeated in Appendix A's notary statute Title 35, though the most relevant and tested parts of it are indexed in ch. 12. There are also several possible pinpoint cross-references *within* ch. 21 which could be added, not detailed here; for example, each kind of land transfer makes reference to "additional provisions for conveyances," so the actual page number, p. 350, should be written at those many reference points (e.g., pp. 334 top, 337 middle, etc.). (Chapters 24 and 25 could be cross-referenced somewhat more than is suggested here, too.) But we do include several cross-references within ch. 19, which is very disorganized.

As with our index (ch. 12), what follows uses some abbreviations, and often does not show the full range of pages for a topic, if the start page is enough since it's clear the discussion continues to the next page.

statutory duty to record 57 ←→ 318 notary duty, party direction, & req'd info

statutory directives for all acts/immovs 59 ←→ ch 19 acts & ch 21 transfers

bonds generally, and for notary 63 ←→ ch 17 suretyships and bonds

incorporeal movables defined 81 ←→ 135 donation of incorporeal movs

prop held in indivision 91 ←→ 546 partition by act ←→ 448 partition by will

usufruct: concept & rules 95-103 ←→ 411 usufr of surviving spouse of decedent ←→ 439 testator may modify/terminate usufruct in a will

donation: concept & rules ch 10 ←→ 347 act of donation: form & content

dation en paiement 128 ←→ 344 form & content for 'giving in payment' act

donation in disguise 133 ←→ 568 cash sales, "consideration," & disguised donation

confirmation of donation 136 ←→ 565 confirmation cures imperfect donation

donation: manual gift of vehicle 134 ←→ 141 + 395 donation of titled movable: AA?

donation: donative intent lingo 140 ←→ 455 same for donation *mortis causa* (will)

fetus as juridical person 160 ←→ 433 fetus as legatee ←→ 409 rule differs if heir

domicile/residence 161 ←→ 300 domicile in authentic act ←→ 539 intent to change

filiation and paternity 163 ←→ 524 acknowledgment of paternity: form & content

tutorship 168 ←→ 447 appointing tutor in will ←→ 539 form for tutorship by will (designation of tutorship) ←→ 311 appearance clause when tutor appears for minor

emancipation of minor 170 ←→ 540 form for limited emancipation by authentic act

community/separate property 178 ←→ 410 community/separate property in estate

matrimonial (antenuptial) agreement 185 ←→ 541 matrim'l agreemt form & content

power of attorney generally ch 15 ←→ 399 for vehicle: to act before OMV

mandatary/agent 230 ←→ 312 appearance clause when appearing for principal

UCC9 security agreemt 255 ←→ 280 combining it as part of collat'l mortg package

mortgage ch 18 ←→ 351 act of mortgage: form & content ←→ 57 duty to record

acknowledged acts 290 ←→ 322 forms of acknowledgment ←→ 388 vehicle title

'full name' in juridical acts 299 ←→ 402 name usage for vehicle title

marital history 302 ←→ 325 marital-status-change decl'tn ←→ 333, 345, 349 req'd

appearance clause in AA 299 ←→ 310 + 321 various forms for appearance clauses

appearing as executor for estate 311 ←→ 406, 441 success'n representative/executor

appearing for partnership, corp, or LLC 311, 322 ←→ 504, 511, 517 those 3 entities ←→ 357 corp resolution or LLC certificate of authority empowers someone to act for "evidence of oath" in act 304 ←→ ch 20 oaths generally & evidence of oath in affid

conclusion of AA 305 ←→ 323 form for conclusion ←→ 423 will attestation clause

signature of party 307 ←→ 312 what constitutes a signature of a party or witness?

incorporating other documents into act 324 ←→ 457 incorporating into a will

affidavit: form & content 330 ←→ ch 27 small succession; 400, 527 act of correction; 529 affid of distinction; 398 affid of heirship

affidavit "sworn to and subscribed" 331 ←→ 540 is named a "jurat," & form for

requirement of paraph for note to mortg, vendor's lien, etc. 356 ←→ 546 forms for paraph & recitation of paraph

affid of one & the same 401 ←→ 529 affid of distinction/affid of identity

accretion of lapsed or refused legacy/inheritance 415 ←→ 478 accretion in trust law

capacity of testator 419 ←→ 452 determining capacity ←→ 433 who can be witness

signing olographic will 422 ←→ 313 no mark allowed to sign will unless notarial ←→ 453 more rules about signing both types of will

providing for disposition of remains (not done if olograph) 423 ←→ 450 notarial will

definition of forced heir & portion 435 ←→ 444 limited power to disinherit/8 grounds ←→ 474 forced portion in trust

forms of trust (inter vivos & will) 464 ←→ 124 no usufruct by donation?; 467 donating property to trust by AA; 449 settlor may modify/revoke i.v. trust in his will

non-legal custodian's affid 543 ←→ 554 provisional custody by mandate

acts in foreign languages 578 ←→ 454 will ←→ 512 + 518 not in articles for corp or LLC ←→ 513 foreign language OK in corp or LLC *name* if English characters

14

Suggested Annotation Holes and Filling Them

These are places in the study guide where there's room for larger annotation beyond some marginal notes. In these places you can write out whole forms of commonly tested acts (donations, usufruct, power of attorney), add bullet-point summaries of the law (e.g., class notes or outlines from a workbook), and have lists of certain rules that can be grouped together, with page numbers (see below, ch. 15).

You're claiming or reclaiming real estate in the book to be able to write extensive notes useful on test day. As is generally true with this book, these tips are not so much about saving time beforehand—it admittedly takes work to create new blank paper and fill it with new material—as about maximizing the chance of passing. And that means being able to quickly see, during the exam, the most common acts and topics you've organized before the exam. Plus the very act of writing acts and notes into your guide is enormously engaged studying that should pay off.

The blank pages (or parts of pages) fall into two camps, depending on how ambitious you are with this concept. First, areas already blank, ready to be annotated. These are visually obvious, so I won't belabor it, other than to share some ideas as to what can fill the space usefully. The ideas are not meant to be exhaustive but just point in the direction you could take it yourself. Second, areas in the guide ideal for whiting out, to create room for more notes and sample acts to have handy. This takes more time but creates more room to do more.

If you do write in notes and acts into your book, which is advisable, be sure to add the page reference to your expanded index. You have to be able to access the samples on exam day.

Before offering some possibilities, let me stress the *essential* one: a general form for most *authentic acts*. Writing this exemplar out by hand is a necessary part of studying, and having it readily accessed during the exam helps answer questions. This is especially so if they, as they often do, give a library document of some act they want you to consider and know its features and flaws. For that, having a viable comparison is crucial. They already do this for you with the *will*: pp. 460-62 and its footnotes provide a good sample. *You* need to do this for the other version of an authentic act, applicable to all sorts of instruments and situations.

Our ch. 8 has the skeleton of a valid authentic act, with some notes on each bone. That needs to be written as a handy part of your guide. In addition, you could write out near it a specific, complete example of an authentic act—such as an Act of Donation of Immovable (this one is best, but more involved) or an Act of Adult Adoption—to illustrate how the bones can be given flesh in a specific context. The one you pick may well be one that gets tested, but even if not, it's a useful example of how such acts are constructed.

The best place to add the outline of components from ch. 8 is the page facing the inside back cover. It's handy on exam day, needs no index to find it, and has plenty of room to write the basic form and notes—such as cross-references, variations, and sample specific language (e.g., an appearance clause if it were a limited emancipation or a mortgage with a confession of judgment). Then there's more room on the opposite page (the actual inside back cover) to insert a filled-out example of an authentic act. We provide a sample donation in our ch. 18.

The *second* most important instrument to write out isn't necessarily an authentic act but does get tested: an Act of Usufruct—assuming you did insert the donation above, which is even more testable. That could fit well on the inside front cover and, if necessary, its facing page (on which you've created room by white-out).

The *third* most important form to insert may be the power of attorney. Near the back of the book (at pp. 652-53), part of the pages just before the authentic-act-form you just added could be used for a sample mandate. This requires whiting-out some of the book's footnotes and endnotes, which don't have testable data on them. Another possible place, at the front, would be pp. ii and iii. We provide a sample power of attorney in ch. 18.

Somewhere on this list of top three or four, you may have already added a sample affidavit to the extra space in ch. 20. We discussed this in our ch. 7. Adding a short one, like our affidavit of translation in ch. 18, will be instructive.

I'd say the three or four above are the minimum forms to add, for real help on the exam. But here are some more places to add more content.

As a possible fifth form, you may want a complete act of sale, somewhere in the book. It could go on pp. ii and iii if you haven't used them up, or near ch. 18 on mortgages (which relates to it somewhat) by using p. 285 whited-out.

Beyond the four or five most useful forms I've suggested above, it seems that the best use of free space would be more specific versions of actual authentic acts (e.g., Act of Correction, Act to Establish Disability, Designation of Tutor), sample trust-creating language, a bill of sale for a car, and a mortgage. You may also want to use free space to write in charts of the differences between various transfers of land (cash sale vs. credit sale vs. act of sale with mortgage, etc.), of the different documents that together create a sale of land with mortgage and promissory note, and a sample promissory note itself.

I've already advised painting room for some sample form at the front, opposite the inside front cover, or using pp. ii and iii. Other areas in the book that can disappear without your caring are suggested below.

- iv, vi, ix
- 3, 4
- 12
- 21
- 77
- 285 (noted above)
- 580, 581
- 652, 653 (noted above)

15

Useful Lists to Insert into the Guide

Without trying to be comprehensive in all the bullet-points one could insert into the guide as notes, this chapter does suggest some key lists that pull together rules or law spread over many places in the book. For example, you saw one such list at the end of our "Acts Required to be in Authentic Form" in ch. 9, and detailed below: four situations in which a power of attorney cannot be used. Rather than indexing the four different places in the book saying this, write all of the four in one place, anywhere, then index just that (as "power of attorney can't be used for, p. xxx,"; also add "mandate can't be used for, p. xxx"). Of course the section on required authentic acts is itself a list compiled from all through the book.

Here are similar useful lists to write somewhere. I also suggest where to write them (matching the index entry), but anywhere is fine as long as you can find it.

1. Situations when social security number or TIN is required as part of appearance clause or similar (p. 303).

7 docs require SS#; first 4 use last 4 digits of *borrower* (=mortg'or):

> 1) conventional mortg
>
> 2) collateral mortg
>
> 3) credit sale (buyer=mortg'or)
>
> 4 any doc creating secur. int. in immov
>
>> + 3 use full #:
>
> 5) TIN of juridical persons in Art. of Incorp. or similar SOS filing
>
> 6) SS# of each parent in act acknow'g paternity, p. 526
>
> 7) TIN of Unincorp. Ass'n in Statement of Authority, p. 359 [include cross-references in list]

2. Situations when a paraph is required (p. 546); but paraph actually goes on Note, see below.

> 1) mortg (conv., collat., etc.); but parties have power to direct Notary not to
>
> 2) sale with mortg
>
> 3) credit sale
>
> 4) pledge

    5) act of partial release

    6) act of subordination [see p. 44 above re its location, or not, in the study guide; you'll likely have to write an insert into the guide itself, and index it]

These require notary to place the *paraph* (starts with "Ne varietur") on the <u>Note</u>, identifying it with transaction. It's a 2-way street (p. 356), requiring "*recitation of paraph*" ("And I,") on mortgage, etc. For paraphing the promissory note itself, see p. 355 ("may be paraphed"—but notary never *signs* note). [I suggest writing this paragraph with the list.]

3. When a mandate or power of attorney cannot be used.

I've added this to the bottom of p. 295 close to its added notes about power of attorney (the notes we add in ch. 9). But I also recommend putting this list near where powers of attorney (mandates and procuration) are discussed, such as p. 224 of the study guide. Add index entries like "power of atty, can't be used for."

    4 things can't be done by POA:

        1) will

        2) affidavit

        3) marriage

        4) adult adoption

4. Recordation rules.

This is done in our suggested index itself (ch. 12 above). Even if you don't insert an index in such detail as this book advises, at least collect all the settings and rules for recordation and filing of acts and other legal instruments (so, write the Recordation entry and page numbers somewhere). Same with the Orleans Parish differences (on recording and more): it's quite testable to place a scenario in Orleans and so make one question turn on the differences that are not found in just one place in the guide. So at least index all pages that distinguish Orleans practice (see our index, ch. 12, under Orleans).

5. When usufructs terminate (p. 99).

    1) at death of usufructary (natural person)

    2) at remarriage (surviving spouse), ordinarily [e.g. testator can extend]

    3) when grant says so, if earlier than death

    4) in 30 yrs or end of juridical person (if juridical person)

6. Authentic acts that also use affidavit form and have components of an affidavit, especially "evidence of oath" and "jurat." This is discussed below in ch. 16, including possible places to list them in your study guide.

16

Ambiguities in the Study Guide

The following are areas of the study guide which may be ambiguous or worded confusingly. Or subject matters where the book seems to leave open a definitive rule. In these instances I provide my best guess below as to how deal with the issue if it's tested, short of "challenging" a question for asking a question to which the study guide gives two answers (they do allow you to challenge questions by a note you include with your answers, though it's not clear that's worth the time). The good news is that they probably won't test on areas where the authors may have realized they were vague on the point. But these are food for thought.

What's in a name? Really, how *full* does it have to be? The notary statute R.S. 35:12(2) (p. 586; also p. 299) says acts require a "full name." But lots of formats really qualify, as the statute makes clear. One that always *fails* is first-and-middle-initials-plus-last, and they're most likely to test that (e.g., in the context of a testament or other authentic act). So, *you can't use J.W. Booth.* But it's also clear that these are all fine: John Wilkes Booth; John W. Booth; J. Wilkes Booth (yes, *that's* a full name). The ambiguity in the law is whether John Booth would be enough. Probably so in real life (certainly so if there's no middle name), and lots of accepted exemplars use just two names in their sample forms; but one *could* read Title 35 as mandating that at least an initial be included if the signer has one.

Signature uses initials instead of writing out full name. Actually, using a full name, above, is not the same as how "full" their *signature* has to be written, which can be quite truncated or illegible (p. 312 of study guide). There's no intended ambiguity here. But it's easy for a student to get "name" mixed up with "signature." Those are really two different components of an act or instrument. Even a "mark" as signature is enough, if intended to act as signing—except for signers of olographic wills and witnesses to a notarial one (pp. 313-14).

Can you use 'Sr.' in a name on an act? Technically, the answer should be "no," since that adds information that is not on the signer's driver's license. Certainly it's "no" for a certificate of title, which needs to track the license exactly (p. 402). In reality people want them on a will or the like to differentiate their son or grandson, and there seems to be no harm. But the exam answer would appear to be "no" in many contexts.

How old does a witness have to be? The general answer seems to be old and mature enough to understand the importance of what it going on (p. 316 of study guide). But the glossary's p. 625 ("Capacity") sets definite minimum ages. It is certainly true, and testable, that the ages for a witness to a *will* are fixed by statute and laid out on p. 318. But for non-will situations, my suggestion is to use the general analysis on p. 316 and not the glossary's summary. At the glossary entry, you may note the discrepancy and cross-reference to the general analysis as essential to check and not rely wholly on this short glossary definition and its 14-year-old rule.

What part of the authentic act is the "evidence of oath" mentioned in chapter 19 at page 304? For most authentic acts *by far*, it's not a part, and really should not be discussed at this point of the book. It's also a bit confusing or cluttered to list it as a component of a "juridical act" on p. 296 at a place in the book where it seems they're talking only about authentic acts or about the typical one. In reality, "evidence of oath" is a component of affidavits and verifications, as ch. 20 makes clearer. The reason the book mentions it in ch. 19 is either because they're trying to be global/generic in talking about all notarial acts, even those not authentic (mainly affidavits), or because there *are* a few authentic acts in the form of affidavits, for which a component is the evidence of oath introduction (and the closing jurat). Crucial examples of hybrid authentic acts/affidavits—not called "authentic affidavits" but you can think of them that way—are:

- *Affidavit of correction (for immovable).* Either by a party or by the notary. See pp. 527-28.

- *Affidavit of immobilization of a movable.* See p. 83, discussing this act as a "declaration" but not quite mentioning that it's an affidavit and that it has to be authentic, too. You need p. 295 to know this. Out of caution, in practice one would make the follow-up *de*immobilization by an "act that transfers ownership," p. 83, also in authentic form. But it would appear that the exam answer for *de*immobilization via an act that ordinarily would not be AA, such as a cash sale, is that it need not be authentic.

- *Declaration of dispensation from collation?* This is mentioned on p. 295 as requiring authentic form. It's also likely to be required to be a valid affidavit, with evidence of oath and jurat. Out of caution, you should certainly construct it that way in practice, and answer any question as though this declaration is, in effect, an authentic affidavit.

Anyway, you may make a note at p. 304 to save "evidence of oath" only for those instruments requiring an oath, and list the above important examples there (and perhaps also at the end of ch. 20).

Small succession affidavits are often written in the form of a true affidavit, though with multiple signers, and then include evidence of oath and jurat. But they can also be authentic acts that expressly state that the signers understand that they make the representations under penalty of perjury. In practice, it's safest to make it a formal affidavit (adding the required perjury clause), and *also* have it signed by two witnesses. The goal is to get it honored by banks, OMV, etc.

Can a bank be a corporation? In real life, yes (though also having to comply with statutes specific to banks). But the "exam answer" seems to be "no," as they use it as a sample answer on p. 648. So, give that answer if asked—most likely in combination with other (non-sampled) answers, such as: Which of the following cannot be organized as a Louisiana corporation? A. bank B. for-profit hospital C. charitable youth recreation league D. investment consulting firm. They seem to want "A." Even so, the guide is ambiguous: on p. 511, it may be that the paragraph is trying to explain they can be corporations as long as they follow specific law on banks.

Can an insurance company be a corporation? This is like the above on banks, though it's not a sample answer in the back of the study guide. Probably they expect the answer "no," by the same reasoning as above, but it's truly ambiguous since, legally, insurance companies certainly may be organized as corporations, but under Title 22. See also p. 500 n.1.

The missing few pages at the end of chapter 29. This omission is noted in our ch. 8, mainly missing verifications and subordination of mortgage. The confusion is likely to be cleared up by the SOS after this book goes to press, either on the website or by adding a page insert to new orders of the guide. That sort of leaves out those who already bought the book, as for the March administration, unless they happen to check the SOS site and see the errata likely to be added there. They'll consider it fair game for testing even if it's not actually in the guide. Luckily, the issues are explained here enough from ch. 8 to answer any likely question, plus the reader is told to check the website for errata and mark any changes into the red book. Don't assume they'll allow you to insert loose pages even of their own errata sheets, unless they clearly tell you so on the website.

The heading at the top of p. 492. The heading "Recapituation" is not introducing a new topic in the study guide; it's just the heading within the document shown. They used a too-large font here and made it seem like a new subject. Similarly, p. 292 indents the paragraph starting at "An act that fails" as if it's part of Art. 1835—when in fact it's text by the study guide authors (using the wrong font).

17

Visualizing Community Property and Wills

The study guide's organization is a bit daunting on the issues raised by wills, successions, and property ownership. There's no real big picture given, so that in ch. 8 you're studying what "things" are, then ch. 12 says how married people own property in Louisiana. There's a little more on marriage agreements in ch. 12 and also 29, then the big payoff in ch. 24: how this affects inheritance (if intestate) or legacies (testate) in a court succession—what other states call "probate." It also affects how small successions work, ch. 27, especially the initial tally of the estate to see whether it's small enough to qualify for succession by affidavit—without court. That's a lot of property-wills-successions spread over five chapters!

Stepping back, the main takeaway is that a succession (whether in court or by affidavit) has to deal with, and finalize the transfers from, the decedent's estate. And that depends on what the "estate" is, which—before that, even—turned on what the decedent "owned" before she or he died. So, the concept of ownership matters, not just when he or she is alive, but also in sorting it out after. The main reason the study guide explains ownership in detail early in the book is not because of how the person owns while alive, but more for what she or he owns—sum total—at the moment of death. That adds up to the "estate," which then becomes a matter for a succession to sort out.

(Well, OK, owning property in community or separately could also matter for donations *inter vivos*, since you can't give what you don't own. You do learn ch. 12 community property law also for the chance that it affects such a donation. But on the exam, property ownership comes up more with testamentary dispositions—the donation *mortis causa*—or as its own set of questions.)

The post-mortem sorting out can be done by operation of law—by the default rules applied to those who died intestate—or can be controlled by the decedent in advance via a will (by what essentially is a donation that kicks in at the moment of death, instead of immediately like with donation *inter vivos*). Having a will gives the decedent not only control over the division of property through succession—perhaps deviating from the default rules of who gets what intestate—but also control over little but important extras that intestate law doesn't deal with at all: naming a tutor for kids, naming an executor to help run the whole thing till the succession is closed, creating trusts for the benefits of others, and even dealing with remains (at least with a notarial will). So, it's a good idea to leave a testament, not just to specify who gets what.

Louisiana pre-decedents can do this in two ways: with an olographic will, or a notarial one. Even those written by attorneys are notarial in the sense that they become real once notarized, whoever drafted it. Guess which version involves the notary, and is most likely tested (and most complicated, so there's more to test). This chapter will be about the notarial will, more than the olographic one or even the default inheritance rules for those without a will—though lots of notarial-will law turns on details of the intestate succession, too.

So, before learning the content and rules for a notarial will, you need to understand the property system. In particular, Louisiana and several other states use community property law (the "legal regime") to govern ownership of things during life and—for our purposes, more importantly—at death. During the marriage, they have much of their property owned together in the sense that they live "in a community of acquets and gains." They may each own separate property, too, according to detailed rules about property that's owned separately while otherwise the couple lives in community and shares much ownership (this is quite apart from a matrimonial agreement that lets them opt out, in whole or in part, of the "legal regime," p. 185, so that they'd be in a "contractual regime").

The following is of course oversimplified, but it does present the big picture (literally), leaving many details to the red book—and many others that guide omits are important for successions in court, or dealing with community property in life, but are not particularly controlled by notaries and not really tested on the exam.

Our discussion will assume, for clarity's sake and not at all because it's necessary or expected, a husband and wife where the husband dies first. They *didn't* opt out of the community property system, and they each have some separate property and share in the community for many other belongings, both movable and immovable. They have children, perhaps under 24 or otherwise subject to the rules of forced heirship—so they can't be entirely cut out of the will. And in fact the husband does have a valid notarial will (maybe the wife does, too, but it doesn't matter in our illustration, since *he* died). His death immediately puts law into action (by seizin, p. 406).

Had he died intestate, all sorts of default rules would control. Many of the same concepts of property ownership and what's in the estate, as discussed below, would apply to his intestate succession, too, mainly differing in who must get the estate. But it does get more complicated since he has a will, in part because he may have redirected the donations away from the default recipients. And because the law of forced heirship, unique to Louisiana among the 50 states, limits his discretion in how much he can redirect away from some kids who would've been heirs had he died intestate. He doesn't have *complete* control, but way more than he'd have without a will at all. He's Adam, and she's Eve.

With that in mind, think of the L-shaped state of Louisiana as made up of three squares. The three also form a rectangle vertically and another one horizontally. For this state, that's a North-South rectangle on the West side, and an East-West rectangle to the South. Mississippi is not part of the equation.

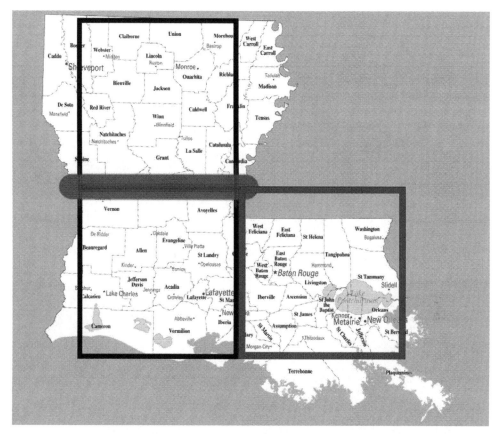

Fig. 1: our state is an L with 3 boxes (or is it 2 rectangles?)

That's the visual. Then there are two important moments in time: while married and Adam's still alive; and at the moment Adam dies. He had executed the will (and the notary "received" it) before he died, but the succession has to divvy up his estate sometime after his death, following the dictates of the will to the extent they followed the law.

The notary's job was to write a valid will expressing the testator Adam's wishes for that moment. The notary needs to understand how property works to implement those wishes. We'll leave it to the succession, usually in court and without a notary's help, to sort out lots more details to finalize the disbursement. For purposes of the exam, the key is to know the law enough to express those wishes validly and to know notary practice enough to write the will competently. Ch. 10, above, was mainly about that drafting task, and that's a lot of what's tested. This is about the law of notarial wills that operationalizes the wishes.

Let's start with the time when they were both alive and owned property—lots of it even owned "together."

Fig. 2: while they're alive and married

Much of the property they own is actually held in community. It's like it's its own thing, though the book stresses it is not a juridical person. It's just a combo of their interests for their "community property." It's shown here as a large swatch of the state, though of course their community property could be a small part of what they each own. But it's a fair characterization because many married couples have, mainly, community property. Each spouse then "owns a present undivided one-half interest in the community property" under the Civil Code (p. 179).

To help visualize this further, and perhaps for you to draw onto page 54's own state map to have during the exam, note that *all* of the parishes that begin with *C* are in or near the western/left side of the state: the community rectangle extends "geographically" from Caddo and the Carrolls at the top, down through many other *C* parishes like Caldwell and Concordia, all the way south to Calcasieu and Cameron. There are plenty more **C parishes** in that rectangular area, too. But there are zero *C* parishes in the southeast corner outside of it.

Adam and Eve hold community property together while married. **CP, like Claiborne Parish or Catahoula Parish, or those many others C Parishes.**

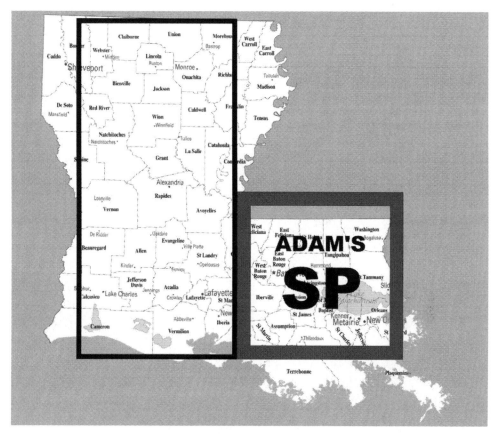

Fig. 3: also while they're married, Adam has some SP

Adam also had some separate property when he was alive and married (not by opting out of the legal regime, but by owning some individually while *also* sharing in the community). He may have inherited a $10,000 Rolex from his uncle, or owned a house before they married that he kept as separate property (which may be challenging because it's pretty easy to commingle the two kinds of property and lose its "separateness"). Eve may have donated her interest in a piece of community property to him, making it separate, p. 182. However it happened, assume that he does own some separate property. It may not be as proportional a part of his total-ownership as the above shows. It could be a big or small part of his total assets. We'll assume the above is accurate enough in this case. It's in addition to that big CP rectangle.

By the way, Eve may have some separate property, too. It might be all of Arkansas, for all we know. It's not really taken into account in the testable part of what happens when *Adam* dies, though. So, ignore the fact that she may really own way more than him, or way more than a half-interest in the CP rectangle. Arkansas is big, but it's Adam's SP that we're concerned with.

Note that almost all of the **nine** (!) parishes that start with *S* are in the southeast quadrant of the state. They start with a "Saint" (Ignore St. Landry, please.) They are the **S parishes. And where the Saints Play. *SP*, like separate property.**

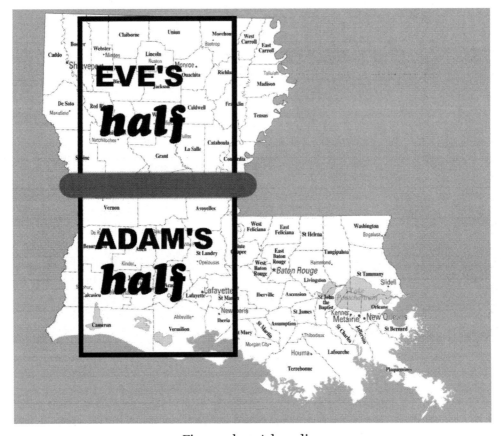

Fig. 4: when Adam dies

At the moment of Adam's sad death from apple poisoning, the community terminates. What used to be community property is now seen as each now owning half of ex-CP. It's not just a half-interest in the whole anymore. It's two separate squares of property now. Eve now owns her half outright.

Assume Eve did not kill him—assume the bad apple came from some other source. Otherwise, she may be an "unworthy successor," to the extent she's a successor at all, p. 417. That would change a lot of the rules, unless he's forgiven her (for an attempt).

Most people think that the surviving spouse is naturally an heir or legatee. Usually not. Follow the rules in ch. 24 as to lines of inheritance to get this. But of course, up to a point, Adam could've provided in his will that she receives his property.

When he dies, his half of the ex-CP property is part of his *estate*. One may describe people as having an estate before they die, of course, and it would've included his *interest* in the CP, but it's when he dies that we care, for test purposes, what's in his "estate." Here, that estate includes his half-share of what used to be CP.

Importantly, *his* estate does not include *Eve's* SP or, more tested, her half of the community that is now part of her own total-ownership we might call *her* estate.

Fig. 5: his whole estate also includes his SP

At the moment of Adam's death, his estate not only consists of his half of the ex-CP property, but also his separate property. His estate could include half of a hunting camp that used to be CP, half a car, and savings they shared—but also SP: that inherited Rolex and perhaps even the house they always lived in. Eve then would not own the house or half the house (unless he lawfully provided so in his will, but assume he did not). It would be to the southeast- or right-side of the map, as SP—but now would be, more importantly, part of Adam's estate as a whole.

(Even if she owns half the house because it *was* CP, she doesn't naturally own the other half. It's part of Adam's estate. Now it'd be to the left of the drawing, in those southwestern parishes that used to be his CP interest. But it's still in the bottom half—in the horizontal rectangle—because it's in his estate. It just got there from formerly being CP, but either way it's part of the estate, and not part of her property.)

The former CP that is now Eve's own property isn't labeled anymore, because it isn't part of Adam's estate. His death without a will doesn't transfer it to anyone, by operation of law. For our purposes, more importantly, her own property—and it's now hers, at the moment of death—is not affected *even by his will* because it's not his to give. Nor can he give away her separate ownership of, say, Arkansas.

Fig. 5 raises all sorts of issues when he has a will, or not. One issue common to those situations is that Eve is not totally SOL. She still has a *usufruct* in the house they shared as community property, if they did, and in any other former CP. She may own half outright, but she has a personal-servitude interest in the other half. Practically speaking, that means she can still live in the house (and use other property) until she dies or remarries, whichever comes first (p. 411). Or he may have a will that changes these rules (p. 439), either in her favor (e.g., extending it past remarriage, or granting a usufruct over his SP), or not (even eliminating the default usufruct).

Under the default rules without his changing them by will, this means that she is the owner of half of the former CP, but there are other, "naked," owners of the other half. They have responsibilities to each other, and many rules apply, but the key for now is to understand what forms part of Adam's own estate. The usufruct that is created by law (or modified by testament) governs her *use* of the property, as detailed in ch. 9, but our focus now is about ownership and what's in the estate.

There's a common test situation where you need to sort out this math: when you're tested on a small-succession question whether the decedent's estate qualifies. Assuming it's not from out-of-state or so old that exceptions apply (p. 495), the total estate of Louisiana property has to be $125,000 or less to at the moment of death. The key is not to include her former CP value in that, or any SP she has. So, if Adam's 10k watch is his only SP, and the house that was CP (his only other possession) is worth $200,000—and there's no will—the heirs can use succession-by-affidavit instead of court. Why? His estate is worth $110,000, which is under the cap.

The issue may also be tested in a direct way without linking it to small-succession eligibility, by asking what Adam's estate is worth in the above example. Answer: $110,000. Read the question carefully, though, since it may make you do the math to include her interest (which isn't the way a court would do it, but they're just making you add the numbers without making it have a legal import). If we include her share, the value of the assets (his estate plus her former CP interest in the one shared asset) is $210,000. These can be tricky, but hopefully sorting out SP from CP and then understanding what's *his* estate at the time of death will make the math simple.

Other than the usufruct, there's other repercussions from the above division of property and its effect on wills and successions. The main one is "forced heirship." We're assuming Adam had children (whether with Eve or otherwise). They were first in line to inherit if there's no will, whatever their age (p. 410). But if there's a will (and only if so), rules of forced heirship kick in. The testator can control, *to a point*, how much of the estate goes to whatever recipient they choose. The "to a point" is forced heirship—a rule that forces a minimum percentage of the estate, whatever the will says, to go to the decedent's living children under 24 (up to that minute, in fact, so: 23 + 364.99 days). Or to those otherwise forced by law (mainly disabled children, whatever their age (pp. 435-36), with even some grandchildren included in exceptional cases). There are only eight, limited grounds on which a testator can override the "force" and disinherit an eligible child (pp. 445-46, often tested).

The above "to a point" and "minimum percentage" may sound ambiguous. No, it's just that the minimum amount—the "forced portion" or "legitme"—varies according to how many children the testator has, especially how many of them are forced heirs (under 24 or disabled and not validly disinherited). For now, assume *one kid:*

Fig. 6: what *must* be a legacy of a forced heir if there's *one*

The lone heir (oddly called an "heir" since this only happens with a will, so shouldn't it be *forced legatee*?) must receive, as the "forced portion," one-fourth of Adam's estate. See p. 435 of the study guide.

The rest of his estate (in gray) is the "disposable portion"—because he is free to donate it to Eve, or Octagon Fighting Club, other children instead, or whoever/ whatever. He could even donate it into a pet trust (p. 479) to the exclusion of the child—up to a point. That point is the forced portion.

Admittedly, now we're getting into the weeds a little. If you understand what is Adam's estate and how CP vs. SP fits into determining that at the time of his death, you're ahead of the game. Most testing should focus on the concept and, perhaps, some math that follows. But be ready for the next-level question: what to do about a forced heir. The simplest such situation involves one forced heir.

The percentages change if there's more than one forced heir. Then the forced portion is one-half of the estate. The testator, Adam, is free to dispose of only half his estate (of which a big part may itself be only half of his former CP). That's limited control. Perhaps it's a good reason to have an only child, or to die after all but one are 24.

Fig. 7: the forced portion if two or more forced heirs

The example is simple, though perhaps tough on Adam's free will (literally), if there are exactly two forced heirs. They split the half of the estate assigned to the forced portion. With three forced heirs: they split the half three ways. But there comes a point where the rules of forced heirship would give one child way too much compared to other, non-forced, children.

The default rules of intestacy would've been fairer to the children *as a whole* if, now that there's a will, one lone forced heir takes over for the non-forced ones (say, several over age 24). That would be youngest-child-syndrome on steroids! We should limit the forced portion of the amazing-super-lucky child—still protected, but only to a point—to the amount he'd receive if Adam *had* died intestate. I say "he" because I'm thinking of Joseph and his jealous, not-so-lucky brothers, though I realize he wasn't Adam's son and this analogy is going off the rails. Anyway, Joseph shouldn't take it all (well, the quarter), just because he's the only forced child—leaving the remaining, unforced brothers with not much left to split, if there are several.

To expand on the example in the study guide (p. 435): where the decedent has five kids, and four are not forced heirs (so the forced portion normally follows Fig. 6, for one forced heir: 25%), the *actual* forced portion is 20%, what he'd get in intestancy. The other children could get less by comparison, but not egregiously so (yes, the four could split the 80% leftover, and equal the forced heir, but also could wind up splitting less if Adam leaves something to the Octagon people or to Eve). Of course, because the 80% is the *disposable* portion, and the four older brothers are not forced, Adam can cut them out entirely, by will. That wouldn't happen in intestancy.

That's the forest of property and testaments, and some trees as well. Most of the details in ch. 24 follow from this structure. What's in the estate is determined from the testator's death, is given immediate ownership to heirs or legatees by seizin, but has to be sorted out as a final matter—to close succession or to allow a succession-by-affidavit—through the rules of intestancy or testancy. If there's a will, there's a place for the notary, both in drafting and in emceeing the authentic act itself. The will must conform to all the formalities and language of an authentic act (and with wording specifically required for such wills, like the attestation clause). But, *stepping back*, the entire concept of donating property after one dies is not just about dotting the i's in a document, it's about dealing with the property as it exists under law. That requires understanding what property is in the estate—and who may receive (and what portion) by default rules of intestancy or, especially, under a valid will.

Fortunately for exam purposes, and even in notary practice, you're not expected to know every nuance, rule, or exception that plays out in court during the succession process. The book in fact warns you not to involve yourself in judicial successions (p. 499), just succession-by-affidavit. You don't need to account for forced heirs when constructing the will—the testator may not know whether they'll have 0 or 12 forced heirs at death, when the determination is made—or for that matter, the value of the estate, then. You just have to have a sense of it to understand the disposable portion the testator truly controls. And know the rules of community property because of the ways they can come up on the exam.

A good grip on the right way to construct a will, consistent with the testator's wishes and a correct sorting of the property at stake, will make the grade. Don't be intimidated.

18

Acts, Forms, and Exemplars

The sample acts and forms provided here aren't meant to be comprehensive. These are some of the main ones likely to be useful on exam day, yet our chapter 16's tips create room in your book to handwrite more than just these. Still, I hope these are a good start, and that by annotating some of them further with marginal notes and the like, they're more useful to understand how these acts, especially the authentic ones, work.

The first isn't the most important or testable one, but it's a fair example of a simple affidavit, yet the study guide doesn't quite provide any other than those related to more core topics such as witness acknowledgments (and none in ch. 20 on affidavits!). Mainly it fits here on a short page, so I've gone ahead and shown one. This could be handwritten onto p. 331, short. Then, one annotated.

AFFIDAVIT OF TRANSLATION

STATE OF LOUISIANA

PARISH OF LINCOLN

BEFORE ME, the undersigned duly commissioned and qualified Notary Public came and appeared the undersigned

PETER GENE HERNANDEZ

who, after being first duly sworn, did depose and say:

THAT he is fluent in the Tagalog language, that he performs under the professional name Bruno Mars, and that the foregoing is an accurate, true, and complete translation of the document attached hereto, entitled "Minutes of Meeting of Corporate Board of Directors, Bank of West Manila, June 12, 2018."

_____
Peter Gene Hernandez, Affiant

SWORN TO AND SUBSCRIBED BEFORE ME

This 9th day of February, 2020

_____
Jamie Lee Curtis, Notary Public
La. Notary ID No. 112233

AFFIDAVIT ← *heading*

STATE OF LOUISIANA

PARISH OF EAST BATON ROUGE → *venue clause (where it's signed)*

← officer before whom statement is made

BEFORE ME, the undersigned Notary Public, duly commissioned and qualified in the parish and state aforesaid, came and appeared the undersigned

RICHARD TIFFANY GERE ← *appearance of affiant*

who, after being first duly sworn, deposed and said: ← *"evidence of oath"*

1. He is of the age of majority and is domiciled in Rapides Parish, Louisiana. *(part of appearance)*

2. [Factual assertion here.] → *core content: the declaration or "deposition"*

3. [Factual assertion here.]

_____ ← *signed in presence of officer (notary) (and that's his actual middle name)*
RICHARD TIFFANY GERE, Affiant
name typed or printed

SWORN TO AND SUBSCRIBED BEFORE ME ← *"jurat" is all-important*

This _____ day of _____, 20____ ← *date of statement (part of jurat)*

_____ ← *notary signature*
Adam Ant, Notary Public ← *name typed or printed*
Bar Roll No. 12345 ← *required (or notary ID #)*
Commissioned for Life

WITNESS ACKNOWLEDGMENT ← *heading*

STATE OF LOUISIANA

PARISH OF JEFFERSON

venue: where executed ("SS" here doesn't mean social security)

just means you verified ID if not personally acquainted

BEFORE ME, the undersigned duly commissioned and qualified Notary Public, came and appeared the undersigned person to me known to be the person described in and who executed the foregoing instrument as a witness thereto and acknowledged that she executed the same as her own free act and deed as such witness.

And affiant, being duly sworn did depose and say that such instrument was executed by the parties thereto in the presence of affiant and the other subscribing witnesses and by all parties thereto of their own free act and deed for the uses, considerations, and purposes therein expressed.

LOUISA MAY ALCOTT, Affiant

jurat

SWORN TO AND SUBSCRIBED BEFORE ME

This _____ day of _____, 20____, at Metairie, Louisiana.

form used to complete an "authenticated act" that was executed by parties who now can't BOTH appear before notary, so: original witness to signing comes in and "acknowledges" the original instrument ...

not quite an "authentic act" but has evidentiary qualities of one (it's "self-proving")

TONYA MAXINE HARDING, Notary Public

Louisiana Notary ID No. 66666

DONATION INTER VIVOS OF IMMOVABLE

(as opposed to "donation mortis causa," i.e., a will)

STATE OF LOUISIANA

venue clause: it's where document is executed, not location of property (or where filed)

PARISH OF ST. CHARLES

BEFORE ME, the undersigned notary, duly commissioned and qualified in the parish and aforesaid, and *preamble*

in the presence of the two witnesses whose names are hereunto subscribed, PERSONALLY CAME and appeared:

[Donor(s) appearance clause(s) reciting (a) full name, domicile, and permanent mailing address of the donor(s); (b) marital status of all donors who are individuals, including full name of the present spouse or a declaration that the party is unmarried; and (c) a declaration as to whether there has been a change in the marital status of any party who is a donor of the immovable or interest or right since (s)he acquired it, and if so, when and in what manner the change occurred.]

appearance clause of donor

Herein DONOR, whether singular or plural who declared that [CAUSE, DEPENDING ON FACTS (e.g., ". . .in consideration of the natural love and affection that he has for DONEE, his nephew," or ". . . in consideration of his support for the improvement of educational opportunities for students of Tulane Law School"),]

such "cause" need not impose conditions

said DONOR did and by these presents does, give, grant, convey, donate, assign, set over and deliver unto

clear intent to give, effective now

[Donee(s) appearance clause(s) reciting (a) the full name, domicile, and permanent mailing address of the donee(s); (b) the marital status of all donees who are individuals, including full name of the present spouse or a declaration that the party is unmarried.]

donee does not have to appear now,

Herein DONEE, whether singular or plural, here present and accepting with gratitude, for himself, his successors and assigns, and acknowledging due delivery and possession thereof, as a donation, the following described property:

but must accept in writing to make effective (usually)

[Legal property description, including the municipal number or postal address of the property if it has one.] *description, not just address*

The parties hereto estimate the value of said donated property in the amount of _____ dollars ($_____ . __ USD), and DONOR declares that the property hereby donated by him does not exceed the disposable portion of his estate.

To have and to hold the said property unto the donee(s), his heirs, successors and assigns, in full ownership forever, with full and general warranty of title, and with full substitution and subrogation to all rights and actions of warranty which said donor may have against all former owners or vendors of said property.

All taxes due on said property have been paid, as evidenced by tax certificate attached hereto. Further tax notices shall be sent to donee at [address].

The parties hereto waive and dispense with the production of any mortgage, conveyance, or other certificates, required by law, and relieve and release me, notary, from any and all connection therewith.

This act is passed before me, notary, without a request for examination of title and none was made. The description herein was furnished to me, notary, by the parties, and the parties relieve and release me from any and all liability in connection therewith, forever holding me, notary, and my heirs and successors harmless from any and all claims forever.

Said donor stipulates that the aforesaid property has not heretofore been alienated by him and is free of all encumbrances.

THUS DONE, READ AND PASSED at my office in the City of Hahnville, Louisiana, on the _____ day of _____, 20____ in the presence of the two undersigned competent witnesses who hereunto sign their names together with said appearers and me, notary.

WITNESSES:

_____   _____ , DONOR

[Type/print W1 name under signature]   [Type/print DONOR name under signature]

_____   _____ , DONEE

[Type/print W2 name under signature]   [Type/print DONEE name under signature]

_____

[Type/print name under signature], Notary Public

Notary ID No. _____

Note: Although the above authentic act assumes that Donee is present and signs, which is typical, the donation may also be completed and effective by the Donee's acceptance later, in writing (usually). Acceptance need not be an authentic act nor necessarily a part of THIS authentic act. If Donee is not present, the above Appearance Clause would be adjusted so as not to say s(he)'s here. In the written acceptance, Donee needs to be clear they are accepting this donation, much like the above. The Study. Guide lists some atypical situations where acceptance is completed by action rather than in writing.

STATE OF LOUISIANA $\rbrace$ *venue clause*

PARISH OF JEFFERSON

LAST WILL AND TESTAMENT

OF

[TESTATOR FULL NAME]

↳ *what constitutes a "full name" & when required? See R.S. 35:12*

BE IT KNOWN, that before me, the undersigned authority, duly commissioned and qualified in and for the Parish of Jefferson, State of Louisiana, and in the presence of the undersigned competent witnesses, personally came and appeared: *preamble: not necessarily required as long as testator's appearance clause appears in his or her statement (after "I")*

[TESTATOR FULL NAME], of the full age of majority, who declared that (s)he lives and resides in the Parish of Jefferson, Louisiana at the following address: [street address, city, LA, zip] *appearance of testator uses residence address instead of domicile, unlike most authentic acts*

who declared to me, Notary, that (s)he wishes to take advantage of the provisions of La. Civ. Code Ann. art. 1576, et seq., and does hereby make and declare this to be his/her last will and testament:

↦ La. courts prefer this to "being of sound mind"

I, [FULL NAME], <u>being able to comprehend generally the nature and consequences of this act</u>, realizing the precarious and uncertain nature of life, and wishing to dispose of all the property which I may own at the time of my death by Last Will and Testament, <u>knowing how and being able to read and write</u>, declare this to be my final testament. I revoke all of my prior testaments or codicils. ↳ *capacity*

I.

Marriage. I, [FULL NAME], have been married twice, first to [NAME], from whom I am divorced, and second to [NAME], from whom I am divorced. I have no minor children or forced heirs. *marital history and current status are also part of T's appearance*

↦ DISPOSITIVE PORTION starts here

II.

A) Specific Bequest. As a specific bequest, I give, will, and bequest the *full and complete ownership* of my box of files to [NAME 1], my granddaughter, so that she may finalize my estate.

B) As an additional specific bequest, I give the *full and complete ownership* of the bank accounts and any stocks in my name to [NAME 2]. ↳ *a particular legacy*

C) I give, will and bequeath the *full and complete ownership* all of the rest of my property to [NAME 3]. If she should predecease me, then the property should go to [NAME 1]. ↳ *universal legacy*

valuable opportunity to appoint one and define duties

III.

A) Executor. I appoint [NAME 1] as Executrix of my succession to serve with full seizing and without bond. Should she cease or fail to serve, I name [NAME 3] as successor Executrix. All of my executors may serve as independent administrators, without court supervision. In accordance with Louisiana Civil Code Article 1572, my executors are authorized to allocate specific assets to satisfy a legacy. All of my executors have my express authority to serve as "independent executors."

signature of T

signature not just initials at end of each page

_____
[testator name]   page 1 of 2

B) Compensation. My individual Executrix shall serve without compensation, but shall be entitled to recover his or her expenses from my Estate.

C) Bond. I dispense all of my Executors, including any duly appointed dative or provisional executor, from giving bond.

D) Selection of Assets. Pursuant to La. Civ. Code art. 1572, my executor has the authority to select assets to satisfy any legacy herein expressed as a quantum or value of my estate, including a fractional share.

E) Common disaster. Should I die together with any legatee in a common disaster or under such circumstances as to render it doubtful as to who died first, it shall be presumed that I survived. *protect against who-died-first*

F) Collation. I dispense all of my heirs from collating any gift received from me whether inter vivos or by reason of my death.

G) Undue Influence. No disposition in this testament has been made by me as a result of hatred, anger, suggestion or captation. I understand the nature and extent of my property and the consequences of the dispositions in this testament.

H) Should any of the provisions of this will be for any reason declared invalid, such invalidity shall not affect any of the other provisions of this will and all invalid provisions shall be wholly disregarded in interpreting this will.

_____ *signature of T*
[Testator name below signature] *type/print full name*

ATTESTATION CLAUSE: Use exact language of C.C. art. 1577, if possible:
In our presence the testator has declared or signified that this instrument is his/her testament and has signed it at the end and on each other separate page, and in the presence of the testator and each other we have hereunto subscribed our names this _____ day of *date is crucial* 20____ at [city], LA.

WITNESSES:

_____ *Signature of W1*
[Witness #1 name printed/typed here]

_____ *signature of W2*
[Witness #2 name printed/typed here]

_____ *Notary's Signature*
[Notary's name printed or typed below signature] *statutory requirements, see R.S. 35:12(B)*
Bar Roll No. 12345
My Commission is for Life

```
STAMP
    TYPICALLY
        HERE
```

page 2 of 2

113

POWER OF ATTORNEY

BY ERIC T. JONES

IN FAVOR OF GREG R. MENDEL

UNITED STATES OF AMERICA

STATE OF LOUISIANA

PARISH OF ST. TAMMANY

BE IT KNOWN that on _____, 20____, before me, _____ _____, a notary public duly qualified in and for the above stated state and parish, and in the presence of the named and undersigned competent witnesses, personally appeared ERIC T. JONES, a person over the age of majority and a resident and domiciliary of St. Tammany Parish, Louisiana, "principal," who declared under oath that he has been married once to Nancy Drew, from whom he is widowed, and has not since remarried, and whose mailing address is 123 Baker St., Abita Springs, LA 70420, and who declared that he appoints GREG R. MENDEL as attorney-in-fact or agent, to act only with consultation of the other and to perform the acts authorized in this power of attorney, hereinafter referred to as "agent," to be his agent, mandatary, and attorney-in-fact, with full power and authority to act for, in the name of and on behalf of principal, to do all acts necessary or deemed by agent to be appropriate to represent principal including, but not limited to, the following:

1. Business and Affairs. To conduct, manage, and transact the business and personal financial matters of principal, of every nature and kind without any exception.

2. Correspondence. To open all letters, emails, facsimiles, and other correspondence, electronic or otherwise, addressed to principal and to answer same in principal's name.

3. Banking. To make and endorse and to accept and to pay promissory notes, drafts, and bills of exchange; to sign checks .... [more on banking actions allowed]

4. Securities. To sell, purchase, and transfer shares of stock, bonds, or any other securities of any corporation or any other legal entity ....

5. Loans. To borrow money in principal's name from any bank or other financial institution; to make, issue, and endorse any promissory note ....

6. Property: Sale, Purchase, Lease, Mortgage, Pledge. To sell, mortgage, encumber, pledge, purchase, lease, or grant servitudes pertaining to immovable (real) or movable (personal) property, although not described in this instrument as permitted by Louisiana Civil Code Annot. art. 2996 on such terms and conditions as determined by agent and to execute such documents to effect such acts and receive or pay amounts pursuant to such acts; this authority and discretion expressly includes the property located at 123 Baker St., Abita Springs, LA 70420, and any automobiles.

7. Judicial Proceedings. To appear before all courts ....

8. Successions. To represent principal judicially and otherwise ....

Page 1 of 3

9. Claims. To demand and obtain and to recover and take receipt for ....

10. Donations. To transfer without consideration (i.e., donate) any asset of principal to any person as determined by agent.

11. Tax Returns and Related Matters. To file any United States, Louisiana or other tax returns (including, but not limited to, income tax returns); to apply for extensions ....

12. General. To do and perform each and every other act, matter or thing as may be appropriate in agent's discretion as if such act, matter or thing were or had been particularly stated in this instrument.

13. Substitute Agent. Principal grants the agent the power to appoint and remove a substitute agent, which appointment will be by authentic act.

14. Liability of Agent. Agent will be liable only for breach of duty to principal committed in bad faith. Principal will indemnify agent and hold agent harmless for all reasonable costs, fees and expenses regarding all matters in this contract, legal actions brought by or against the agent for which agent is not liable within the standard specified in this section. No further compensation shall be allowed.

15. Reliance. This power of attorney and any substitute power of attorney executed pursuant to Section 17, above, may be filed and recorded with the clerk of court for Jefferson Parish and registered in the conveyance records, and will remain in effect as to third persons dealing with the agent until either the power or substitute power of attorney is revoked by notarial act and recorded as set forth above, and/or the third person receives actual notice of revocation. If any party who relies on this power of attorney delivers written notice to the principal, this power of attorney will remain in effect until the party receives written notice of revocation, notwithstanding recordation of revocation as stated above.

THUS DONE AND PASSED, on the day, month, and year first above written, in the presence of the undersigned competent witnesses who have signed their names together with the principal and me, notary.

I understand the full import of this designation, and I am emotionally and mentally competent to make this appointment and grant these powers and authorities.

_____

ERIC T. JONES, Principal

Witnesses:

_____   _____
Witness signature   Witness signature

_____   _____
Printed name of W1   Printed name of W2

Notary Printed Name _____
Notary ID Number _____

The undersigned accepts the appointment created by this power of attorney to act as the principal's true and lawful agent, mandatary, and attorney-in-fact.

_____

GREG R. MENDEL, Agent

CERTIFICATE OF ACKNOWLEDGMENT OF NOTARY PUBLIC:

State of Louisiana

Parish of St. Tammany

On this, the _____ day of _____, 20____, before me _____, personally appeared Eric T. Jones, personally known to me, whose name is subscribed to this/these instrument(s) and acknowledged to me that he executed the same in his authorized capacity, and that by his signature on the instrument, executed the instrument. I declare that he appears of sound mind and not under or subject to duress, fraud, or undue influence, that he acknowledges the execution of the same to be his voluntary act and deed, and that I am not the agent (attorney-in-fact), proxy, surrogate, or a successor of any such, as designated within this document, nor do I hold any interest in his estate through a testament or by other operation of law.

Any person, entity, hospital, credit union, institution, court, or agency may rely on a machine copy of this instrument that is certified to be true by the Notary Public before whom it was originally executed.

WITNESS my hand and official seal.

_____

Signature of Notary Public

Notary Printed Name _____
Notary ID Number _____
My Commission is for Life

BILL OF SALE OF A MOVABLE

STATE OF LOUISIANA
PARISH OF _____

BEFORE ME, the undersigned Notary Public, duly commissioned and qualified in and for the parish and state aforesaid, personally came and appeared:

_____ ,

Seller, of legal age, who hereby sells and delivers with full and general warranty of title unto:

_____ ,

Buyer, of legal age, the following movable property:

Make:

Model:

Year:

VIN:

Vehicle Sale Price: Date of Sale:

Seller warrants that there are no mortgages, liens or encumbrances of any kind against the movable property sold or any accessories attached thereon.

Signed on this _____ day of _____, year of 20___.

signed here _____
Seller
signed here _____
Buyer

_____
_____ (print name),
Notary Public, ID # _____

19

Notarial Practice Tips

Once you've passed and received your commission, here are some practice tips or answers to day-to-day questions that the study guide does not fully share. For that reason, not all of the advisories below will be on the exam (though they bring a practicality to some transactions and forms that they may help you remember items that *are* in the study guide and get tested). At least, you may want to have these suggestions around when you do start your career as a practicing notary, or are already qualified as one due to bar membership. My wife Michele and I have learned them mainly through our notary practice and asking around, or through books we've read (some listed in one of the items below).

Your signature is your seal. But. The study guide does make clear that no more than your signature is required to complete the notarization process (p. 71). That fact has been tested, probably because it's counterintuitive that a state so steeped in formalities and ritual is fine with a less-formal seal than most states use. The guide suggests that end-users, especially out-of-state recipients of notarized documents, don't *know* that a signature is enough (also p. 71). Or their state law won't allow a mere signature. So they may reject the forms. For this reason, notaries have official stamps and embossers made and keep them handy (such as a second set in the car). Moreover, clients *expect* them, even Louisiana ones.

Where to get stamps. Quality and affordable stamps and embossers can be found from many local rubberstamp companies (like Ed Smith Stencil Works in New Orleans), online notary stores, and even Amazon. We've found from word-of-mouth and experience that Trodat brand embossers fit better in your hand than most other inexpensive brands. A paired stamp and embosser run about $39 online. Mail-order embossers tend to be a bit tricky to assemble, in that you may think the device is properly seated when it really isn't.

Other stamps. In addition to the basic stamp that has your name, parish, state, and notary ID number, practitioners find it useful to get a few made that they use a lot more than they'd guess. One is "A True Copy" stamp, to certify copies of documents you've originated (pp. 535-36 in the guide). Another is a jurat stamp ("Sworn to and subscribed..."; see p. 540) that pretty much turns a client's letter or statement they've prepared into a mini-affidavit, at least sufficient to satisfy a school, landlord, sporting league, or other entity that wants a notarized statement of fact (such as a statement of residence address) and is not looking for a formal courtroom-style affidavit.

Certified birth certificates or official records. You can't make a "true copy" of birth certificates, death certificates and the like—that's up to the bureau of vital statistics (p. 538). So, what to do when a school or recreational organization requires "a notarized birth certificate"? Or someone similarly is looking for an official record to be certified? The ready solution, which satisfies most such requests, is for the client to state that it is an exact copy and sign that statement, and for you to use the jurat stamp (or a jurat you write onto the copy) to show that they have sworn to the fact before you. Adding your signature and your notary stamp should suffice. Although you can probably also make the copy yourself and notarize your own statement that you copied it accurately (in essence only swearing that it's a good copy, not that the original is valid, see p. 537), the safer route is to state it in the form of the client's own brief affidavit. By the way, you can't legally photocopy at all some naturalization documents (they say so on the paper), much less certify them as a true copy.

What do "seal" and "SS" mean on a form? Many forms that require notarization have a special place marked "seal." Sometimes that means "signature," like where it's just a line. Yet they are probably looking for an actual stamp or embossing, not just your signature (despite Louisiana law, above). To be cautious, most practitioners use both stamp and embossing in that spot, and physically sign the form too on the appropriate line. As for "SS," usually found near the venue clause, that's not asking for a social security number; it's short for a Latin phrase that means "namely" or "to wit," and can just be ignored.

What if a form asks for the end-date of my commission? Forms often do, because all other states have limited terms. Don't leave the line blank (after "Commission expires ___"), or they may think yours expired. Fill in "with life," or "with death." (My wife sometimes writes in "when I do.") Some stamps and stock forms say it, too: "My Commission is for Life," below the notary's name/ID number. If they *insist* on an end-date, I guess you could name a distant one?

Where do I emboss if there's no space for it? NOT over the signatures, dates, or other features that are meant to be part of the notarization ritual. Use the margin if you need to, and at worst emboss over some unimportant words in the document. If there's room, ideally the stamp and/or embossing go below your signature; some sources say the best place is to the left side of the page, below the signature.

What if a document is meant to be faxed or scanned after notarization? The embossing alone won't show well after scanning and the recipient may think it was not stamped. Using both a stamp and an embosser solves the issue. Some use a different, round stamp that looks like inked embossing (and don't further emboss it). Others use a gold, round label stuck to the paper and then emboss over it. Most likely the basic (rectangular) stamp is fine.

What if you make an error on a document a client brings you? This will happen. It's best to make a copy before working on anything halfway complicated, or at least ask if the customer has the original in an email they could access (so it can be recreated if the first one is marred, for instance by writing the names in the wrong place). White-out is never allowed. If the document is a certificate of title, there's a detailed (and tested) process using an affidavit of correction (pp. 400-01) that must be done for all errors, even small ones, or just to strike out something goofy on the back. For less official and immutable documents, usually a cross-through correction by the notary, initialed by the notary, will fix it.

What if the form says "County of" instead of "Parish of"? You certainly *could* cross out the word and replace it with the proper Louisiana unit. Many notaries routinely do and they're right to say the document remains valid. But we've found that some out-of-state recipients of documents they don't want to honor quickly (such as a lien release that means the recipient now has to pay a contractor) may look for any excuse to say the form was altered and is no longer valid. We suggest not crossing it out but simply filling the blank with, say, Caddo Parish or just Caddo. It's odd to say "County of Caddo Parish," sure, but the form will always be honored. This is like the fact that "your signature is your seal": you know that's law, but if the recipient doesn't believe you, what good is being right? Similarly, don't insist on teaching a recipient a geography lesson when the only goal should be to have the notarization recognized.

What if the client has signed the form before they see you? They often think they are doing you a favor, or saving time, to go ahead and sign it before you see them. If they have another original they can sign in front of you, that's ideal, but it's usually satisfactory to have them sign the form again in your presence (even at the bottom of the page). The book provides case law (p. 330) that suggests a signer of an affidavit can *confirm* their signature to you if they already signed it. But really there's no reason to create an issue when it's possible to have them sign the document in your presence even if they signed it previously.

What if the client signs as an agent or mandatary on behalf of a principal? Be sure to instruct them to sign the document with their own name, and not "forge" the principal's name on the signature line. It's intuitive to clients that the form is asking for the principal's name to be signed, even if they have to do it "for" the principal. But that's wrong, and they probably need to be specifically told to sign their own name before they put pen to paper—and invalidate the form, which may be the one copy they have.

What to do if they don't have one of the listed IDs? Page 71 lists the four forms of ID which suffice (unless you know the client well, or someone you know well vouches for their identity, in which case they can forego ID). If they don't have that ID, don't assume they are who they say they are. The easiest ways to commit professional malpractice are to allow a signer to talk you into ignoring their lack of ID or to fail to have the person physically in front of you when they sign.

Where to check out-of-state identifications to be sure they're real? There are huge books sold, expensively, that cover all sorts of identifications with pictures and updates. For almost all notary purposes, though, Google is your friend and does the trick.

Forms that say "personally known to me" when I don't know the person? For most forms, that just means that they became personally known to you because you checked the appropriate ID above (or actually do know them). They don't expect you to attest to signatures only of people you knew before they came through the door. Other forms, more helpfully, list in the alternative "personally known to me *or* identified by _____" where you are expected to fill in the blank with "LA driver's license" or similar (or underline "personally known" if they really are, then cross a line above their blank line, so you don't make it seem like neither applies). We make a practice of filling in not only the form of ID but the number on it ("LA driver lic 2751662") so that the user *knows* we checked.

Blanks in forms? You're not supposed to let the form be signed before its blanks are filled in (pp. 573-74). That seems most crucial in cases where the missing information is something they are attesting to, and not just informational like their phone number. In any event, the end product needs to have blanks filled in, with lines to show the blank was considered but ignored, or use of "N/A" and "none" to explain the omitted data. Certainly you can't notarize essentially a blank form or document, especially with affidavits, authentic acts, and other instruments where the signing is the last part of the ritual that makes it legally valid.

Using ordinals in filling in dates? It's not necessary to write the *th* in "6th day of June, 2019" when filling blanks in acts or forms by hand. The 6 alone will do. We do tend to write 1st instead of 1, just because the lone mark may look like it's not fully marked in, so adding some characters there makes it clear it's the 'first.'

Take your time. Don't be afraid to ask a client to come back after you've researched and drafted the matter rather than trying to impress them by doing it on the spot. Even with a form the client brings in, use the red book and its sequels to look up a subject area rather than going on memory. Of course you'd recall when confronted by two parents and a baby that the state form for acknowledging paternity is an authentic act. But without looking at the guide's section on this monumental moment (p. 524), you may not recall that you have to read, and give in writing, specific disclaimers to the parents, if not the baby.

Organizations to join. Both the Louisiana Notary Association (LNA.org) and the Professional Civil Law Notaries Association (PCLNA.org) are excellent professional groups which offer continuing education, newsletters, legislative updates, forms, and networking. It appears that the live seminars or meetings they routinely offer are geared more for northern Louisiana with LNA and southern Louisiana with PCLNA, but really both groups have members statewide.

Where to get more forms and exemplars? Comprehensive sets of forms, acts, and examples for almost any situation can be purchased from many sources, including downloadable sources, and in notebook form from the Louisiana Notary Association (their latest *Notary Survival Kit*). All sorts of forms, bills of sale, and sample acts can be found online with a search. And resources of various prep courses (such as the excellent PassMyNotary workbooks and iNotaryNow notebook) include many of the most used forms. In all cases, be sure you are using a form that is for Louisiana. Other states are too different.

Other books to have handy. In addition to the *Survival Kit* or similar resources that provide many forms (at least downloadable and readily available from some reputable source), and of course the *Fundamentals* guide and this book, consider having a recent edition of the Louisiana Civil Code on your shelf. The LNA offers one by a leading law publisher—West—at a discount price for members. We also recommend a brief, clear, and inexpensive book (at Amazon and the like): Gregory Rome and Stephan Kinsella, *Louisiana Civil Law Dictionary* (2011). The National Notary Association's *Notary Home Study Course* is actually a useful book to read as you embark in the profession—surprisingly: (1) much of its advice is useful even in Louisiana, especially as to the attesting-to-signatures part, and (2) despite its title, it's not so much about studying for a future exam as it is about the day-to-day work of a notary on a very practical level.

Should I notarize a will that a customer brings to me that seems to be prepared from an online resource or providers like LegalZoom? Probably not, unless it's clear that it meets all the requirements of Louisiana testamentary law and accomplishes what the testator intends. You're not doing them any favors by notarizing a will that isn't going to be valid but will add an extra layer of litigation or doubt over having no will at all. Sure signs that they don't get that we're different is when they use the common law phrase "being of sound mind"—or, far worse, they have the testator initial the bottom of pages instead of signing, as Louisiana law absolutely requires. Just say no.

Wrong signer? It's fairly common for clients to think they're the one to sign the form when it's supposed to be their spouse (as with the consent by non-participant spouse to allow a withdrawal from a retirement plan) or parent (as with a mom's guaranteeing payments to a college residence). Or they think that one of them can sign it at home and the other bring it to the notary. We've found that the children in the residence-guarantee situation are often quite insistent that the form was signed by their parent and don't seem to understand that the point of a notary is to *see* it be signed. There's nothing you can do in such situations but insist, politely, that the correct signer come by.

Negotiation of pricing. Many customers think there's no reason a notary should charge money, especially if they're from other states where notary services are often provided free at banks. The civil law notary is much more than the notary in any other state and deserves to be paid for their professional services. Have a standard, printed-out list of prices for particular services, and stand by it. When clients try to self-discount their particular need from your standard prices (many try), it's tempting to give in, but it's not right—and it tends to become permanent even if you made clear it's a one-time favor. Do it only if there's some larger need of yours that you're serving (such as offering it free as part of a larger transaction for which you're charging), not just as a favor or the path of least resistance. Have a way to accept credit card payments or provide change and receipts.

Don't get suspended. It's embarrassing, though easily fixed, to be suspended because you haven't filed an annual report or otherwise remained technically eligible (such as being actively registered to vote, or renewing your bond). A casual review of actual notary listings on the Secretary of State's website reveals that very many of the non-attorney notaries have been suspended for a brief period at one or two points of their careers. You need to calendar the earliest time that your annual report may be filed and have your phone alert you as well. Don't ignore emails and letters from the Secretariat.

Get E&O coverage and not just a bond. Professional failures and mistakes can occur even if you never mean to. It doesn't cost much more beyond the surety bond (which protects the Governor) to get Errors & Omissions protection for yourself. Typically a bond bought online—it's easy, from many companies—costs about $110 for five years, while an E&O policy (that satisfies the bond requirement, too) is $140 to 150, so we're talking $8 or less difference per year. It may actually save money, as discussed above at the end of ch. 4.

The most important tip is in the study guide. On p. 557 and elsewhere the guide suggests that the easiest way to lose your commission and your reputation is to deviate from rules you know to be the case—as by doing someone "a favor," such as notarizing forms dropped off to you already signed by someone not before you. We've had people ask us to confirm over the phone that they gave permission to have someone bring the form by. Maybe they can be forgiven for not understanding what a notary is for. You won't be. Every time you're asked to cut a corner for an employer or customer, remind yourself how challenging this journey is. If you have to, say to *them*: "You have no idea what someone has to go through to become a notary in Louisiana. The exam has a 20% pass rate and cost a lot. I'm sorry I can't risk losing that for you." If they don't understand *that*, it's a big red flag that maybe they're trying to get you to cut corners for suspicious reasons and not just because they left their ID at home.

Some other very important tips are not. Be professional, be patient, never put yourself into a physically (not just legally) vulnerable position, take pride, and have fun.

About the Author

STEVEN ALAN CHILDRESS is a senior professor at Tulane Law School, holding the Conrad Meyer III Professorship in Civil Procedure. He has taught Evidence, Torts, and The Legal Profession at Tulane since 1988, in addition to visiting positions at Loyola–New Orleans and George Washington. He has lectured in Tulane's continuing legal education program on notary law and practice, legal ethics, and Louisiana evidence law, as well as teaching Louisiana Bar Review for a decade.

Alan earned his law degree from Harvard and a PhD in Jurisprudence from Berkeley. He clerked in Shreveport for the federal court of appeals, then practiced law in California with two national firms. He is a member of the Louisiana Notary Association, the Law & Society Association, and the California and D.C. bar associations. He coauthored the three-volume treatise *Federal Standards of Review*, edited two books on legal ethics, and annotated a 2010 edition of Oliver Wendell Holmes' *The Common Law*.

He is a commissioned Louisiana notary with statewide jurisdiction who, with his wife Michele (an attorney-notary since 2002), owns a notary/shipping service in Jefferson Parish, seen at *www.mailandnotary.com*. He's in the relatively rare position of having taken both a bar exam and the notary exam.

If you have suggestions for test-taking advice, corrections to this guidebook, reflections about current exam topics, or examples where you think the author's strategies can be improved, please email them to: *achildress@tulane.edu*.

qp

Visit us at *www.quidprobooks.com.*

Made in the USA
Columbia, SC
24 February 2020

88287203R00074